BETTER
to
MARRY

SEX AND MARRIAGE
in
I CORINTHIANS 6 & 7

Appendix: The Remarriage

of the "Innocent Party" — A Sermon

David J. Engelsma

REFORMED FREE PUB.   ASSOCIATION
Grand Rapids, Michigan

Library of Congress Catalog Card Number:
93-85593
ISBN 0-916 206-49-1

Printed in the United States of America

#30671187

For Ruth

*But if they cannot contain,
let them marry: for it is better
to marry than to burn.*
—I Corinthians 7:9

TABLE OF CONTENTS

Introduction

There is great need for a faithful witness in the churches of the West to the biblical teaching on the related subjects of sex, marriage, divorce, remarriage, and single life. Western civilization shows its fundamental paganism by its unashamed promiscuity and perversity. A disciplined, holy life regarding sex and marriage is not only crumbling in the churches, but also has in many churches already completely broken down. The impure and disorderly lives of the members meet with silence on the part of the churches' teaching office. Or the churches defend and justify the sexual uncleanness and marital infidelity of their members. Either the churches officially adopt reports that sanction the sexual activity of the unmarried, the unbiblical divorcing and the remarrying of the married, and the homosexual lust and conduct of married and unmarried; or the churches preach a grace of God in Christ that approves all this wickedness by tolerating it in the lives of professing Christians and in the fellowship of the congregation.

None of this is due to any fault in the Scriptures. The Scriptures speak clearly, sharply, and extensively on those aspects of the holy life of the believer that consist of sexual purity and of the sanctity of marriage. One of the outstanding passages is I Corinthians 7.

As is indicated by the words that introduce the chapter, "Now concerning the things whereof ye wrote unto me," the apostle is answering specific questions about marriage from the recent converts in Corinth, Greece. These new Christians had problems in their marriages and problems with marriage itself. Like all good pastors, the apostle is forced to be a marriage counselor. The chapter, therefore, is primarily practical. It differs in this respect from that other great passage in Paul's writings on marriage, Ephesians 5:22ff., which is primarily doctrinal. However, the apostle answers the practical questions and solves the problems by applying the doctrine of the Word of God to the lives of the Corinthian saints. He does not accommodate the holy life of the believers in marriage or in single life to the prevailing culture in Corinth. He does not make concessions because of the situation of his questioners. He is not pragmatic, interested in what "works." Rather, he shows and insists upon the practice required by the gospel of Jesus Christ.

Like the Corinthians, the people of God at the end of the twentieth century must seek answers to their marriage problems from the apostles of Christ, that is, from the Word of God. Like the apostle, the churches must give the Word of God as the answers to these problems. The world is filled with advice and counsel about sex and about marriage. But the world's wisdom in these matters is not derived from the gospel of Jesus Christ. Listened to, this wisdom leads the saints astray. It is foolishness. It becomes increasingly rare that the churches and their teachers base their instruction and guidance squarely on the Word of God. Especially when church members find themselves in marital difficulties, the churches are ready to give counsel that deviates from, and even plainly contradicts, Holy Scripture. In the end, there is no difference between the advice of the unbelieving counselor and the advice of the supposedly Christian marriage counselor.

Christ has His own unique practice of marriage. Therefore, the church, taught to observe all things that Christ commanded the apostles (Matt. 28:20), has her own distinctive counsel concerning problems in this important area of human life.

Paul's answers to the questions of the Corinthians became part of the apostle's open letter to the entire congregation at Corinth and part of the inspired Scriptures to the church of all ages. This, evidently, is instruction that all need and that all may have — married and unmarried, men and women, adults and children.

The presence of the seventh chapter of I Corinthians in the Bible guards against two dangers into which churches can fall. One is that the churches keep back sharp, strong teaching on marriage from their members because this teaching will offend some or because it will make the lives of some very painful. This is common. As divorce and remarriage become rampant in almost all churches, the preachers see to it that they never proclaim God's hatred of divorce (Mal. 2:16) or the adultery of remarriage (Mark 10:1-12). It is a striking thing that often it is the very people whom the preachers are trying to protect who are dissatisfied with the churches' silence and who demand to know what the Bible really teaches.

Besides, if the churches teach faithfully, they can to a large extent prevent the sins and miseries that now are flooding the congregations.

The apostle was not hesitant to give the recent converts at Corinth the full, plain, unvarnished truth about marriage, even though for some this meant a difficult, painful life. Some had to remain married to unbelievers. Others had to remain unmarried as long as they lived.

The other danger warded off by the presence of I Corinthians 7 in the Bible is that the churches neglect to teach certain aspects of marriage because of squeamishness about sex.

The Scriptures are characterized by frankness and openness about sex both as regards its abuse outside of marriage, e.g., Proverbs 5 and 7, and as regards its use and enjoyment within marriage, e.g., Proverbs 5 and the Song of Solomon. Paul is open and blunt in I Corinthians 7. The subject of verses 2-5 is the sexual aspect of marriage and sexual behavior in marriage. John Calvin took note of this in his commentary on I Corinthians 7:5:

> Profane persons might think that Paul does not act with sufficient modesty in discoursing in this manner as to the intercourse of a husband with his wife; or at least that it was unbecoming the dignity of an Apostle.

The churches also must be free to speak plainly and unashamedly about sex, especially since the saints at the end of the twentieth century live in an impudent world. Yet, like their apostle, the churches may not trifle with the subject in a silly, jesting, crude, or embarrassing manner. The church has her own spiritual manner as well as her own sound message.

We must also learn from the answers to the Corinthians' questions about marriage, what truths about our own marriages are important. We must learn to ask the right questions. It is a real danger today that Christians learn their questions from the world. "How can I be happy in marriage?" "How can I find the greatest sexual pleasure and satisfaction?" "What may I do to deliver myself from the misery of a bad wife or husband?"

The Scriptures teach believers to ask their own, and quite different, questions. "In what calling am I to please God — in marriage or single life?" "How can I please my wife or husband sexually?" "If I have a miserable wife or husband, what am I required by the

Lord to do in order to honor His marriage ordinance?"

In this book, the Scriptures will control the questions as well as the answers.

Chapter 1
Flee Fornication

Flee fornication ... he that committeth fornication sinneth against his own body.
— *I Corinthians 6:18*

Immediately upon taking up chapter 7 of I Corinthians, we are directed to the background of the chapter in the warning against fornication in I Corinthians 6:13-20. The reason given for marrying in verse 2 directs us to this background: "to avoid fornication" (literally: "on account of fornications").

In the New Testament, fornication (Greek: *porneia,* from the word for a whore) does not refer only to the sexual sin of unmarried persons before marriage. Often, it refers to sexual sin of all kinds whether committed by unmarried persons or by married persons. In Matthew 5:32 and in Matthew 19:9 "fornication" refers to illicit sexual activity on the part of a married person. In Ephesians 5:3 it is used broadly to include all forms of transgression against the seventh commandment. Moulton and Milligan's *The Vocabulary of the Greek New Testament* explains "fornication" as "applied to unlawful sexual intercourse generally. It was a wider term than *moicheia* (the Greek word for adultery — DJE)."

Defending the explanation of "fornication" in Matthew 5:32 and Matthew 19:9 as "extra-marital intercourse on the part of the wife, which in practice is adultery," the *Theological Dictionary of the New Tes-*

tament rejects the interpretation that makes "fornication" sexual sin prior to marriage as though "fornication" in the New Testament always refers exclusively to sexual activity of the unmarried.[1]

The fornication against which Paul warns in I Corinthians 6 was intercourse with whores not only by the unmarried men of the Corinthian congregation but also by the married men.

Fornication Is Common

This was so common in the pagan world of Paul's time, and especially in Corinth, that nothing was thought of it. It was accepted behavior like eating and drinking. For this reason the apostle had to insist on a radical difference between eating and fornicating: "Meats for the belly, and the belly for meats: but God shall destroy both it and them. Now the body is not for fornication, but for the Lord: and the Lord for the body" (I Cor. 6:13). The prevalence of fornication among the heathen and the heathen attitude toward it of taking it for granted were indicated by the decision of the Jerusalem Council in Acts 15. This decision had to mention the sin of fornication, with certain matters of Christian liberty, as forbidden to the converts from heathendom.

In the fornicating world of that day, Corinth was notorious for sexual license. It was the San Francisco of that time. F. F. Bruce has written that Corinth's "name became proverbial for sexual laxity. The verb *corinthiazesthai*, lit. 'to play the Corinthian,' was current

---

[1]   Gerhard Kittel and Gerhard Friedrich, ed., Geoffrey W. Bromiley, trans. and ed.,*Theological Dictionary of the New Testament* (Grand Rapids: Wm. B. Eerdmans Publishing Company, 1964-1974), 6:592.

from the fifth century B.C. in the sense of practising fornication."[2]

As the decision of the Jerusalem Council made plain, it was a danger that Gentile converts to Christianity, having adopted the attitude of their society toward fornication, would carry that attitude with them into the church. They would then not view fornication as diametrically opposed to the Christian faith and life and as absolutely forbidden to disciples of Christ. Rather, they would regard it as something permitted to Christians and, therefore, would freely practice it. It was particularly the danger that these converts from heathendom would view fornicating as their freedom in Christ. This made it necessary that the apostle address the issue of Christian liberty in I Corinthians 6:12: "All things are lawful unto me, but all things are not expedient: all things are lawful for me, but I will not be brought under the power of any." Verses 13ff. make clear that fornicating is not a matter of Christian liberty. Fornicating is sin: "He that committeth fornication sinneth against his own body" (v. 18). It is a gross and grievous sin against the Lord Christ and His gospel.

This points out that the situation of those to whom the Holy Spirit addressed I Corinthians 7, with its background in the condemnation of fornication in chapter 6, was the same as the situation of the saints today. Christians today live in a world saturated with fornication. It is no different from eating, except that more effort is put forth to stir up the appetite for fornicating than for eating. The result is that, at best, the members of the churches are inclined to view fornication indulgently. At worst, they practice it as an activity for which

---

[2]   F.F. Bruce, *Paul: Apostle of the Heart Set Free* (Grand Rapids: Wm. B. Eerdmans Publishing Company, 1977), p. 249.

the gospel of Christ gives them liberty. This is found in churches that are evangelical and Reformed. Baptized young people fornicate freely, if not boldly, all the while maintaining their membership in the churches and thinking of themselves as Christians. If it has not come to such a pass that married church members visit the whores or sleep with other men than their husbands, as their freedom in Jesus, married professing Christians do publicly practice fornication as a gospel-right by divorcing their mates and remarrying the object of their lust.

Fornication Is Condemned

The apostle of Christ breaks into this situation with the gospel's uncompromising condemnation of fornication and sharp warning against this sin. Here is evident both the moral purity of the gospel and its fearless courage, as well, of course, as the courage of the genuine preacher of the gospel. Christianity opposes the prevailing culture! The gospel is the sworn foe of sexual immorality! The true servant of the Lord makes no concessions to the fornicating age, offers no compromise with the world's thinking on fornication, and licenses no church member's fornication by appeal to the liberty of the gospel of grace.

The condemnation of fornication begins already in verses 9-11 of I Corinthians 6.

> Know ye not that the unrighteous shall not inherit the kingdom of God? Be not deceived: neither fornicators, nor idolaters, nor adulterers, nor effeminate, nor abusers of themselves with mankind,
> Nor thieves, nor covetous, nor drunkards, nor revilers, nor extortioners, shall inherit the kingdom of God.

> And such were some of you: but ye are
> washed, but ye are sanctified, but ye are justified
> in the name of the Lord Jesus, and by the Spirit of
> our God.

Fornicators will not inherit the kingdom of God in the Day of Christ. One specific form of fornication which, if impenitently continued in, will exclude those who have practiced it from the kingdom is homosexual activity ("effeminate ... abusers of themselves with mankind"). In verse 11 the power of the gospel to cleanse men and women from fornication is extolled. It forgives all past sins of fornication, including homosexual sins ("but ye are justified ..."); and it breaks the ruling power of the sin of fornication ("but ye are sanctified ..."). Whether the gospel has the power to deliver those who have the perverse desire for people of their own sex, so that they crucify this desire and resolutely refuse to practice it, is not even a question in the church where the gospel is known. The "name of the Lord Jesus and ... the Spirit of our God" have this power in every child of God who may have this unnatural desire, just as they have this power in the other children of God who struggle with natural sexual lusts.

The condemnation of fornication, stated in verses 9-11, is fully worked out in I Corinthians 6:13-20. The starting-point of the careful exposure of fornication as unlawful for the Christian is the fundamental truth that the body of the Christian shares in the redemption of Christ: "ye are bought with a price ..." (v. 20). Because the believer has been bought with the blood of Christ, body as well as spirit, his body belongs to God: " ... which are God's" (v. 20). It follows that the body of the believer is "for the Lord (Jesus)", even as "the Lord (is) for the body" (v. 13). The believer's body has the glorious, everlasting destiny of the resurrection (v. 14).

No less glorious is the present condition of the body. The believer's body is the dwelling — the "temple" — "of the Holy Ghost" (v. 19). By this indwelling of the Spirit, who is the Spirit of Christ, the body is united to Christ so that the body as a whole and every member in particular, including the sexual organs, are "members of Christ" (v. 15).

The Christian is "joined unto the Lord (Jesus)" (v. 17), and this "joining" includes the body. The word in the Greek is *kollaoo*. It is the word translated "cleave" in Matthew 19:5, with reference to the one-flesh union of husband and wife in marriage, as originally revealed in Genesis 2:24: "A man ... shall cleave unto his wife ...." Every believer is joined to Christ with his body, because Christ cleaves to him, body as well as soul, in the mystery of the real, spiritual marriage (cf. Eph. 5:22ff.).

This makes fornication an appalling, repulsive, almost unthinkable sin. The fornicating Christian unites the members of Christ with the whore: "Shall I then take the members of Christ, and make them the members of an harlot?" (v. 15).

There is no such thing as "casual sex." According to verse 16, the fornicator is *"joined* (Greek: *kollaoo)* to an harlot." The fornicator does not merely "have sex" with a whore (who can be the professional prostitute or the "easy mark" at school or the adulterous woman in the neighborhood). But in the sexual act he is joined to her, cleaves to her, enters into a relationship with her that is something like the union of marriage.

This last is expressed when the apostle states that the fornicator becomes "one body" with the whore, on the ground ("for") that God said that the "two ... shall be one flesh" (v. 16). The apostle does not teach that sex with a whore constitutes marriage. Deliberately, he describes the relationship with the whore as "one *body*," not as one *flesh*. Becoming one flesh is a marriage. Becoming one body is not. Nevertheless, there is a union that parodies that of marriage. Because fornication uses sex in sinning, sex that belongs strictly, exclusively, and significantly to marriage, sex that is at the heart of marriage's unique union, every act of fornication involves a real, a close, and a significant union of the two. There is a shadow-union of marriage, a devilish counterpart to, and imitation of, marriage.

The horror is that the Christian does this with a body that is united to Christ so that now Christ is united to a whore through the fornicating Christian.

Against this, Paul reacts with his strongest expression of outrage and disgust: "God forbid" (v. 15). If the churches today are unable to make this "God forbid" their own, in their preaching and discipline, there is no love for Jesus Christ in them, nor any honor of the risen, all-glorious Lord.

Running from Fornication

Because of the utter "unbecomingness" of fornication for Christians and because of the prevalence and power of the temptation to fornicate, the apostle calls the saints, old and young, to "flee fornication!" (v. 18) This is a far stronger admonition than the demand not to commit fornication. Many sins the Christian ought to stand up to. This one even the holiest saint must run away from. The only way of conquering is the way of the abjectest cowardice. A brave man or woman here is a fool.

The saint flees by avoiding whatever incites to fornication, whatever could conceivably lead to it, and whatever is remotely connected with it. This includes dangerous physical proximity and contact, e.g., dancing. Banned are all books, magazines, and pictures that present fornication as good and that stir up the passion of illicit sexual desire—a desire that is powerful enough without any artificial incitement. The English word "pornography" is derived from the Greek word for fornication, *porneia*, indicating that this shameful product of a debauched culture (which some professing Christians evidently suppose they have the liberty to enjoy) falls directly under the vehement denunciation of the apostle in I Corinthians 6. Prudent obedience to the command to flee fornication is a reason why the Christian does not watch many programs on television and most of the movies. Indeed, it is a reason why Christians ought seriously to consider not having a television set in their home. It is difficult to flee fornication when almost every program and every commercial trades on fornication and arouses unchaste thoughts and desires.

In addition, the child of God flees fornication by running into marriage. This is the connection between the warning against fornication in I Corinthians 6 and the advocacy of marriage in I Corinthians 7. To avoid fornication, let every saint marry.

A Unique Warning

Before we look at chapter 7's instruction regarding sex in marriage, several observations on chapter 6's warning against sex outside of marriage are in order.

First, the warning is timely. This is so obvious to everyone that nothing more needs to be said about it.

Second, the warning is clear, sharp, and urgent.

Third, the warning is uniquely the warning *of the gospel*. It is a warning to believers and their holy children based on their status as redeemed, renewed saints in

Christ. It is not a warning to all and sundry because fornication ruins society and because fornication exposes physical life to deadly diseases. But it is a warning to those whom Christ bought at the price of His blood and in whom the Holy Spirit has taken up His abode (and who know themselves as such), because fornication dishonors their Lord Jesus, His Spirit, and His God. The question for the Christian, which alone has the power to keep him, or her, from the pleasure of fornication, is not "Shall I risk AIDS, or pregnancy, or disgrace?" but "Shall I then take the members of Christ, and make them the members of a whore?"

This must be the approach of parents and churches with their young people. There is some place in this instruction for warning about the peculiar judgments of a holy God upon the body and earthly life of the fornicator. Proverbs 5 makes this plain. The father warns his son that if he fornicates with the strange woman he will "mourn at the last, when thy flesh and thy body are consumed" (v. 11). But the sex education of godly parents does not consist of recommending condoms to our sons and of helping our daughters obtain birth prevention pills. It is rather the teaching of the gospel, "Your body is for the Lord; therefore, glorify God in your body."

Sex outside of marriage is forbidden Christians as the grossest form of dishonoring the Lord Jesus. Fornication makes a cuckold of Jesus. It joins the holy Jesus to a filthy whore.

This condemnation of fornication forms the backdrop of the apostle's instruction concerning marriage in I Corinthians 7. The absolute, unqualified prohibition of sex outside marriage serves the legitimization, indeed the advocacy, of sex within marriage.

Chapter 2
Pay the Debt

Let the husband render unto the wife due
benevolence: and likewise also the wife unto
the husband.... Defraud ye not one the other....
                                            — I Corinthians 7:3, 5

The subject in I Corinthians 7 is marriage, specifically the behavior of Christians with regard to and in marriage. The apostle is led to this subject by practical questions concerning their marriage problems from the members of the church at Corinth. The first question had to do with sex. This is apparent from Paul's opening answer: "Now concerning the things whereof ye wrote unto me: It is good for a man not to touch a woman" (v. 1).

Some Christians questioned whether Christianity did not really forbid marriage altogether and whether it did not require single life. They were of that opinion because marriage is so "fleshly," so "unspiritual," on account of the "touching" of sex. Their question went something like this: "Paul, would it not be good for us spiritual Corinthian saints to avoid marital relations entirely? Should not the single be commanded not to get married? And should not those of us who are married separate or arrange a 'Joseph marriage'?"

Sexless Marriage

A "Joseph marriage" is a marriage without sexual

relations. The name is derived from the Roman Catholic description of the marriage of the mother of Jesus and her husband Joseph. In the interests of their doctrine of the perpetual virginity of Mary ("*Virgo ante partum, in partu et post partum,*" "a virgin before birth, in birth, and after birth"), itself a doctrine intended to support and encourage the worship of Mary by Roman Catholics inasmuch as virginity is supposed to be inherently more holy than marriage, Rome teaches that Joseph and Mary never had sexual relations. "Sexual intercourse was not an essential element in marriage, which continued to be a full marriage even when sexual intercourse played no part. The marriage of Mary and Joseph was the 'perfect marriage.'"[3]

Rome's view of virginity as an intrinsically higher spiritual state than marriage is expressed in The Canons and Decrees of the Council of Trent, Twenty-Fourth Session, "Doctrine on the Sacrament of Matrimony," Canon X: "If any one saith ... that it is not better and more blessed to remain in virginity, or in celibacy, than to be united in matrimony: let him be anathema."[4]

Mary's perpetual virginity is confessed by Rome in many places. Article IX of the Profession of the Tridentine Faith (1564) speaks of "the perpetual Virgin the Mother of God."[5] The Apostolic Constitution of Pope Pius XII (1950), *"Munificentissimus Deus,"* declaring it to be Roman Catholic dogma that Mary was assumed into heaven, body and soul, calls Mary "the ever Virgin Mary": "We pronounce, declare, and define it to be a divinely revealed dogma: that the Immaculate Mother

3   Edward Schillebeeckx, *Marriage: Human Reality and Saving Mystery* (London: Sheed and Ward, 1965), p. 291.
4   Philip Schaff, *The Creeds of Christendom* (New York: Harper & Brothers, 1890), 2:197.
5   Schaff, *Creeds,* 2:209.

of God, the ever Virgin Mary, having completed the course of her earthly life, was assumed body and soul into heavenly glory."[6] In its "Dogmatic Constitution on the Church," the Second Vatican Council (1963-1965), quoting the Canon of the Roman Mass, declares that "the faithful must also venerate the memory 'above all of the glorious and perpetual Virgin Mary, Mother of our God and Lord Jesus Christ.' "[7] Thomas Aquinas thinks it necessary to "abhor the error" that dares to assert "that Christ's Mother, after His Birth, was carnally known by Joseph, and bore other children. For, in the first place, this is derogatory to Christ's perfection.... Secondly, this error is an insult to the Holy Ghost .... Thirdly, this is derogatory to the dignity and holiness of God's Mother.... Fourthly, it would be tantamount to an imputation of extreme presumption in Joseph, to assume that he attempted to violate (sic!) her ...."[8] Mary's perpetual virginity had been made part of the confession of the fifth ecumenical council, II Constantinople (A.D. 553): "the holy and glorious Mary, Mother of God and always a virgin."[9]

There is no biblical evidence whatever for a perpetual virginity of Mary. Luke 1:27, 34 teaches the virginity of Mary at the conception of Jesus, not a lifelong condition of the mother of Jesus. The Scriptures refute the Roman teaching of Mary's perpetual virginity and the fiction of the "Joseph marriage." Matthew 1:25 implies that Joseph did "know," that is, have sexual

---

[6]   Washington, DC: National Catholic Welfare Conference, n.d., p. 19.
[7]   Walter M. Abbott, ed., Joseph Gallagher, trans. ed., *The Documents of Vatican II* (New York: The America Press, 1966), p. 86.
[8]   *Summa Theologica*, Pt. III, Q. 28, Art. 3.
[9]   Philip Schaff and Henry Wace, ed., *A Select Library of Nicene and Post-Nicene Fathers of the Christian Church,* Second Series, Volume XIV, *The Seven Ecumenical Councils,* Henry R. Percival, ed. (Grand Rapids: Wm. B. Eerdmans Publishing Company, n.d.), p. 312.

relations with, Mary after Jesus' birth: "And knew her not till she had brought forth her firstborn son." To escape this implication, the Roman Catholic Bible translator Ronald Knox deliberately mistranslated, "And he had not known her when she bore a son, her firstborn." Matthew 13:55, 56 teaches that Joseph and Mary had four sons and at least two daughters after Mary gave birth to Jesus (cf. also Mark 3:31-35). This is offensive only to the church that is determined to break the first commandment by worshiping Mary and even then only if that church has a fundamental problem with the gospel's message that sex as a "creature of God is good, and nothing to be refused, if it be received with thanksgiving: for it is sanctified by the word of God and prayer" (I Tim. 4:4, 5).

The Evil of Asceticism

In Corinth, as in the early church generally, there was a tendency to disparage, and even forbid, marriage. The apostles had to contend with the morbid creation-denying and world-fleeing heresy of asceticism. The apostle fully analyzes and roundly damns this "doctrine of devils" in I Timothy 4:1ff. As I Timothy 4:3 shows, a characteristic feature of this anti-Christian philosophy is that it is always "forbidding to marry." This found permanent expression in Roman Catholicism with its celibacy of the clergy as the implication of its teaching that marriage is intrinsically unspiritual and that the single life, therefore, is inherently more spiritual and more holy than marriage.

One of the things that Paul must do in this outstanding chapter on marriage is to teach the fundamental doctrine that marriage is lawful; pleasing to God; perfectly honorable for all Christians; and, as a rule, the necessary mode of life for all Christians, clergy and laity, if they wish to avoid fornication. He affirms God's institution of marriage as a sexual union in creation (cf. Gen. 2:18ff.). He reminds the saints of Christ's approval of marriage in Matthew 19:3ff.

The apostle begins in I Corinthians 7:1b by conceding to the questioner that it is good for a man not to touch a woman. That is, for an unmarried man to refrain from sexual relations by never marrying is both permissible and, under certain conditions which Paul will mention in verses 7-9, preferable. The man for whom it is good that he not touch a woman sexually is an unmarried man. It is good for him to remain single, not as though the single state is holier than the married state, much less as though the single state is holy in contrast to evil marriage, but in the sense that the single life is an excellent, useful way of life for some Christians.

Nevertheless, single life is not the rule for Christians, but the exception. Ordinarily, the will of God for Christians is marriage. The apostle, therefore, exhorts the members of the church to marry: "Let every man have his own wife, and let every woman have her own husband" (v. 2). The reason is "to avoid fornication" (v. 2). The increased sexual desire of male and female is satisfied in marriage. Marriage is the earthly solution to the temptation of fornication.

This seems a prosaic, even ignoble, reason for marrying. It is not that the young man and the young woman want to reflect the union of Christ and the church. It is not even that they are attracted by romantic love. They are to marry "on account of fornications." Similarly, in verse 9, the apostle gives as the reason for marrying that for some who "cannot contain," that is, control their sexual desire, it is "better to marry than to burn."

Is the apostle in fact teaching that marriage is a "necessary evil," as the early church fathers held?

What the apostle teaches elsewhere about marriage must fill out the total picture of marriage as presented by Paul. Particularly, what the apostle teaches about marriage in Ephesians 5:22ff. must not be forgotten when one reads I Corinthians 7. The apostle who elsewhere is idealistic about the marriage of Christians, proclaiming it in the lofty terms of a symbol of the covenant between Christ and the church, is here very practical, down-to-earth, and indeed earthy in his description of marriage. Nor is this earthy description of Christian marriage unworthy of the apostle, or in the least at odds with the idealistic description in Ephesians 5:22ff. There is a perfectly healthy realism about the Word of God. It is practical wisdom to recognize the power of the sexual nature and desire. It is an honoring of God's work of creation to call Christians to marriage as not only the remedy for sexual burning but also the goal of the sexual nature of men and women as creatures of God.

The implied warning to those members of the church who deliberately refuse to marry for wrong reasons should not be overlooked. Some decline to marry because they enjoy the earthly freedom of single life and shrink from the responsibilities of marriage. The warning is that they are likely to fall, or run, into fornication. As a rule, the alternative to marriage is not celibacy but fornication. In view of the dreadful wickedness of fornication, as pointed out at the end of I Corinthians 6, this alone is good reason to marry.

A Celibate Clergy?

Disregarding this clear warning, the Roman Catholic Church has forbidden marriage to all its clergy.

Rome, therefore, is directly responsible before God for the fornication that has always been and is today endemic to their clergy from priest to pope. Even the secular media in recent times have been noting the widespread sexual immorality, especially the homosexuality, of the Roman clergy. Many instances of sexual immorality are dragged into the light of public knowledge. Much more remains hidden until the things done in secret are publicized in the final judgment. And this does not yet take into consideration those who, although they may refrain from sexual relations with others, "burn," to use the language of I Corinthians 7:9, that is, are constantly on fire with sexual passion.

This wickedness of the Roman clergy should surprise no one who has read I Corinthians 7:2. It is one of the truly humorous aspects of church history that Roman Catholic polemicists rail against the Protestant Reformation as an unchaste movement *because the Reformers advocated marriage for the ministers.* Luther, who well knew the uncleanness of the Roman clergy, ironically called attention to the Roman Catholic position in his commentary on I Corinthians 7:

> But even though one were to defile a hundred married women, corrupt a hundred virgins, and keep a hundred whores at one time, still this man can be a priest, become or remain a priest — so remarkably holy is this priesthood! No sin or shame is so great or so widespread in the whole world as to prevent a man from being or becoming a priest, except the state of holy matrimony .... This one work of God has no place in the priesthood.

Dropping the irony, Luther went on to judge the Roman law of the celibacy of the clergy in sober truth:

> And what do they expect to achieve by this, if not
> to defame the divine institution of marriage and
> pave the way for fornication throughout the world?
> And this is what is happening before our very
> eyes....[10]

John Calvin commented similarly on the Roman
Catholic charge against the Reformers that "we have
stirred up something like a Trojan War on account of
women." Calvin was referring to the Roman assertion
"that Luther and others, urged on by the itching of the
flesh, not only created the freedom of marriage for
themselves but also dragged a multitude of priests,
monks, and nuns into the same allurements." Noting
significantly that he would say nothing about the "unnatural lusts" that had free play among the Roman
clergy, Calvin responded, "Certainly, to put it at the
lowest, it is not necessary to go outside the papacy for
those who like women." This is about as much humor
as Calvin allowed himself in his writings.[11]

It is better to marry.

The Goodness of Sex

Within marriage, sex with its intense pleasures is
good. As the Holy Spirit declares in Hebrews 13:4, in
honor of His own work, sex fully partakes of the honorableness of marriage.

> Marriage is honourable in all, and the bed

---

[10]   Hilton C. Oswald, ed., *Luther's Works,* Volume 28 (St. Louis:
Concordia Publishing House, 1973), p. 24.
[11]   John W. Fraser, tr., *Concerning Scandals* (Grand Rapids: Wm. B.
Eerdmans Publishing Company, 1978), pp. 102-106. For an account of the
Roman Catholic polemic against the Reformation as a sensual movement,
confer James Atkinson, *Martin Luther: Prophet to the Church Catholic*
(Exeter, Devon: The Paternoster Press, 1983), pp. 3-20.

undefiled: but whoremongers and adulterers
God will judge.

Christians may enjoy sex with full right and perfect
freedom. However, also here, a certain distinctive,
uniquely Christian viewpoint must prevail.

This is the remarkable instruction of verses 3-5 of I
Corinthians 7.

> Let the husband render unto the wife due
> benevolence: and likewise also the wife unto the
> husband.
> The wife hath not power of her own body, but
> the husband: and likewise also the husband hath
> not power of his own body, but the wife.
> Defraud ye not one the other, except it be with
> consent for a time, that ye may give yourselves to
> fasting and prayer; and come together again, that
> Satan tempt you not for your incontinency.

The Duty of Sex

Whereas prior to marriage it is good that a man not
touch a woman sexually, after a man has married,
abstinence is no longer good. Some married Corinthians,
it will be remembered, were of a mind that the abstinence of married Christians would be a good thing
because the sexual relationship is beneath the dignity of
truly spiritual people. The apostle does not so much
refute this notion as demolish it by the startling assertion
that sexual intercourse is a *duty* for married Christians.
Sex is a "debt" that the husband owes his wife and a
"debt" that the wife owes her husband. This is clearly
implied by the admonition in verse 5, "Defraud ye not
one the other." One defrauds another by not giving him
what is owed him.

That sex in marriage is a debt is expressly stated by

another reading of verse 3 than that which appears in the King James Bible. The King James has, "Let the husband render unto the wife *due benevolence* ...." The reader probably understands this to be a general kindness of word and deed that is obligatory upon husbands and wives. The other reading has, bluntly, "Let the husband render *the debt* ...." With this reading, there can be no misunderstanding the apostle's meaning: Within marriage, sex is a debt that each owes the other.

The meaning of the text is the same regardless of which reading is adopted. If we retain the reading of the King James Version, the reference of "benevolence" is not to kindness in general. The mention of "benevolence" in verse 3 occurs in the context of the treatment of the sexual aspect of marriage. Verse 1 establishes the subject of a man's touching a woman. Verse 2 requires marriage to avoid fornication. Verse 4 gives husbands and wives authority over the body of their mates. Verse 5 forbids married persons to withhold themselves from their mates sexually. In this context "benevolence" cannot refer to kindness generally but must refer to the sexual activity. This is a particular act of kindness springing from the love that the husband has for his wife and that the wife has for her husband. Also on the reading of the King James Version, this sexual kindness is "due," that is, owed — a debt.[12]

In sexual intercourse, each "pays off" the debt he or she owes the other. The word in verse 3 translated

---

[12] The Greek word translated "benevolence" by the King James Version in I Corinthians 7:3 is *eunoia*. Although the *Theological Dictionary of the New Testament* does not even consider the word as appearing in I Corinthians 7:3, since the *TDNT* recognizes the other reading as the correct reading of the text, it does, interestingly, note that *eunoia* is used "sometimes for sexual union," inasmuch as it can refer specifically to the "love between husband and wife." References are given to secular authors. Cf. *TDNT*, 4:972.

"render" literally means "pay off that which is owed."
The attitude of the married Christian, therefore, may not
be that sex is a favor that he or she graciously bestows
upon the other. Sex is a marital duty. Now it may be
more than a duty. Indeed, it ought to be more than a
duty. The Song of Solomon sings sex as a delightful
pleasure that the husband and wife enjoy. But sex may
not be less than a duty.

Paul is opposing a false and wicked spirituality that
is not unknown in the church. Husbands and wives
have left their mates in order to serve God in a more
spiritual vocation. Or they live together, but one or the
other refuses sexual relations because sex is carnal.

At the same time, the Word corrects believing men
and women who neglect, or refuse, to live sexually with
their mates for all kinds of other reasons. There are
marriages, there are occasions in marriage, there are
such strains upon marriages that make this command
crucially important for the salvation of the marriages of
the saints.

The ground of the exhortation "Pay off the debt" is
that married people now have authority over each
other's body. This is verse 4: "The wife hath not power
of her own body, but the husband," etc. "Hath ...
power" is literally "has ... authority," "has ... rights in."
The husband's body is no longer exclusively his own. It
is now also his wife's. The same is true of the body of the
married woman: It belongs also to the husband.

Underlying this assertion of mutual rights in each
other's body is the fundamental truth about marriage
laid down by the Creator in the beginning: "And they
shall be one flesh" (Gen. 2:24). Husband and wife are no
longer two but one. So intimately close are they, such is
the divine fusion, that there are no longer two bodies but
one male/female body. Such is the union of marriage

that neither may say about even his or her body "mine." But each must say "ours."

Because sexual intercourse is a debt owed, inasmuch as married persons have authority over each other's body, for one to withhold himself or herself from the other sexually is "defrauding" (v. 5). This is the same word that is used in I Corinthians 6:7 of the stealing of property or money. The husband who allows himself to lose interest in sexual relations with his wife or the wife who always has a headache is a thief, a defrauder. They are in a class with all deadbeats who do not pay their debts and thus steal from those to whom the debts are owed.

Sexual Abstinence in Marriage

The one exception to the prohibition of abstaining from sexual relations is "with consent for a time, that ye may give yourselves to fasting and prayer" (v. 5). Abstaining must be mutually agreed upon, not unilaterally imposed. It must be only "for a time." It may not be permanent. Nor may it be an indefinite period. The limit must be set. It must be for a spiritual purpose: "Fasting and prayer."

Despite the noble spiritual purpose, the time of abstinence may not be prolonged: "And come together again, that Satan tempt you not for your incontinency." "Incontinency" is literally "lack of self-control." Satan will tempt married persons who abstain for too long a time. One or the other may prove to be unable to restrain himself or herself so that he or she falls into fornication.

The apostle is a realist. He knows the power of the sexual desire. He knows the weakness of the saints. He knows that the great enemy of the people of God is on the prowl seeking to devour them by means of the sexual desire. Satan has an interest in the sexual behavior of the saints as well as in their doctrinal beliefs. He places his agents in the bedrooms of the Christians as well as in the theological halls of the churches.

The striking exception to the rule of living together sexually, consisting of a short period of fervent prayer, brings out two intriguing practical truths about the sexual relationship of married Christians. First, such is the purity, the goodness, the honorableness of sex that it can easily and without any embarrassment consort with prayer. The husband and wife get up from their knees, where they have been worshiping God intensely, to renew their sexual relationship with equal intensity.

Second, the exception in favor of prayer and fasting clearly indicates that the spiritual aspect of the shared lives of married Christians — their worship of the God and Father of Jesus Christ — must both be present in marriage and have precedence over the physical, sexual aspect. The same is taught in I Peter 3:7, where the apostle Peter gives as the purpose of a husband's living rightly with his wife, "that your prayers be not hindered."

How many believing husbands and wives have recently abstained from sexual relations for a time in order to give themselves more ardently to prayer? How many have ever done this?

The ignoring of the provision that sexual relations be interrupted for "prayer and fasting" should not lightly be laughed off. Christian marriage is in dire straits at the end of the twentieth century. In many evangelical churches the rate of the breaking up of marriages is the same as in the world around the churches. And the rate is high, scandalously high. Invariably, the break-up of a marriage means that one or both of the married persons has fallen, or will fall, to fornication. But the threat to marriage in the churches is not mainly sexual. It is spiritual. For solid, healthy, Christ-honoring, and, yes, happy marriages, the spiritual life shared by husband and wife is basic — the life of worship, of the reading and study of Scripture, of seeking to do the will of God, of dealing at once with sin's influence upon the marriage and home. And for this vibrant, strong spiritual life, prayer is necessary, prayer intensified, perhaps, by temporary abstinence from food and from sex.

Important Implications

This inspired instruction about sex in marriage has several important implications.

First, the apostle of our Lord limits sexual intercourse strictly to the marriage relationship: "Let every man have his own wife, and let every woman have her own husband" (v. 2). Outside of marriage, every sexual relationship is fornication.

Second, within marriage, sex is good and of great importance. It is not shameful, but neither is it of trifling importance. It is of great importance both for the extremely important avoidance of fornication and for the extremely important expression and enjoyment of the unique intimacy of the marriage bond. The sexual union of husband and wife is of great importance altogether apart from producing children. Procreation is not the only purpose, nor even the primary purpose, of sex. Much less is it true, as some of the church fathers thought, that sex is redeemed and justified by the begetting of children. That which God has made and the gospel has blessed needs no "redemption" and "justification."

Third, the gospel has its own unique viewpoint regarding the activity of sex in marriage. Relentlessly, the gospel brings its demand that the Christian live, not for himself but for his neighbor into the sexual relationship. Husband and wife must view themselves as belonging to the other. Each then must have the concern and determination to please the other, rather than exclusively, or even mainly, to gratify himself or herself. This is the force of verse 3: "Let the husband pay off the debt owed to the wife ... likewise also the wife ...." This viewpoint on sex is the exact opposite of the viewpoint of human nature: "Let the husband take from the wife what he can get; likewise, let the wife gratify herself by the husband." The gospel's viewpoint on sex is that one gives rather than gets and that one pleases the other rather than gratifies himself.

Failure to practice this is the cause of serious trouble in marriage. The husband ignores the sexual needs and desires of his wife, is inconsiderate of her different make-up as a female, and pleases himself by means of her. He uses her. Or the wife, giving no thought to her husband's sexual wants, regulates their sexual relationship simply by her own feelings. She forgets him.

Fourth, although husband and wife have authority over each other's body, this authority must be exercised in love, as all the rights of Christians must be exercised. Neither may abuse or force or humiliate the other. In Ephesians 5:28 the apostle calls on the believing husband to nourish and cherish his wife. Implied is that married couples speak freely about the sexual aspect of their marriage and, particularly, about the pleasing of each other in the sexual relationship.

Fifth, this marvelous intimacy — a good gift to Christians from the Creator and a gift sanctified to the use and enjoyment of the saints by the Redeemer — points to the essential truth about marriage, namely, that marriage is a one-flesh bond.

But before we consider this, we must hear what the apostle of Christ says about single life.

Chapter 3
Abide Even As I

I say therefore to the unmarried and widows,
It is good for them if they abide even as I.
— *I Corinthians 7:8*

I Corinthians 7 is the outstanding passage in the Scriptures on the practical aspects of marriage. The reason is that the apostle is answering questions from the Corinthian Christians concerning problems they faced in marriage: "Now concerning the things whereof ye wrote unto me" (v. 1). The apostle of Christ, who has such a lofty view of Christian marriage in Ephesians 5, seeing it as the symbol of the heavenly covenant between Christ and the church, here gets "down to earth." He gives instruction concerning various practical aspects and problem-areas of marriage. Even the reasons he gives for his exhortation to the men and women in the church to marry are earthy, realistic, and practical: "To avoid fornication" (v. 2) and because it is "better to marry than to burn" (v. 9).

So must the church be practical about marriage in her preaching, her teaching, her writing, and her counselling. This is one of the most urgent demands upon the church at the end of the twentieth century when marriage after marriage breaks up and when many other marriages suffer severe strains.

Not Advice but Law

Because the passage is "merely" practical and because it "only" has to do with certain problems in everyday life, we may not, therefore, take the passage lightly. We may not regard it as mere advice, and probably as advice that was good only for that time and that culture. For, first, all of the instruction that Paul gives comes straight out of the fundamental, unchanging, and unchangeable truth about marriage that he expresses at the conclusion of the passage in verse 39: Wives and husbands are bound to each other as long as they both live. This is the principle, the basic, God-established truth regarding marriage.

In the church of Christ, practice is determined by principle. The preacher exhorts the practical matters of Christian life "which become sound doctrine" (Titus 2:1). The elders discipline according to the standard whether the member denies God and occasions blasphemy of His Word by his works (Titus 1:16; 2:5). This is not, in fact, how it goes in many churches. Today, practice is permitted to set aside and abolish the fundamental biblical principle concerning marriage. But this only reveals the reality and extent of the falling away, the becoming cold of the love of many, and the abounding of lawlessness in the last days foretold by the Scriptures (II Thess. 2:3; Matt. 24:12).

We ought not take the practical instruction lightly, in the second place, because the apostle expressly states, several times throughout the passage, that what he teaches is the commandment of the Lord Jesus, binding upon all Christians everywhere. Concerning the prohibition against wives leaving their husbands and husbands putting away their wives in verses 10 and 11, Paul writes, "I command, yet not I, but the Lord."

At the end of all that he has said in I Corinthians 6:9-7:17 about fornication, sex in marriage, the rule that Christians marry, the exception that some remain single, and the forbidding of divorce; the apostle writes in verse 17, "And so ordain I in all churches." What he has said on these matters is not "mere advice" but a laying down of law, as the binding rule for Christian life, by the apostle of Christ. Also, all of his instruction is ordained "in all churches." It was binding for all churches in all the world at that time. It is binding for all churches today.

A third reason for taking this practical instruction seriously is that the dark background of it all is the threat of fornication. Contrary to the notion that is found even in the churches today, fornication is no trivial matter. Impenitent fornicators will be excluded from the kingdom of God (I Cor. 6:9,10). For a Christian, fornication is joining Christ to a whore (I Cor. 6:15ff.). The urgent admonition to every child of God, married as well as unmarried, is "Flee fornication!" (I Cor. 6:18).

In his marriage instruction, the apostle reminds us that the threat to those who ignore his instruction is the vile, shameful, cursed sin of fornication. This is the warning of I Corinthians 7:2 where he gives as the reason for marrying "to avoid fornication." Verse 5 warns that failure on the part of married Christians to live together sexually will mean that "Satan (will) tempt you ... for your incontinency," that is, tempt one or the other to fornicate.

One takes the teaching of I Corinthians 7 lightly at his peril. The peril is mortal.

Implied is that the apostle's instruction in the passage about single life also be taken seriously. This too is the authoritative Word of Christ to all churches.

The Single Christian

If I Corinthians 7 is the outstanding passage in the

Scriptures on the practical side of marriage, it is also the outstanding passage on the single life for some Christians. It is safe to say that Reformed Christians have generally failed to do justice to what the apostle says about single life in this passage. They have, therefore, failed to do justice to the single life that some of their members actually live and that others might live, if properly instructed. There are two main reasons for this failure. One is the strong reaction on the part of the Reformed against the Roman Catholic use of this passage to support its teaching that the single life is inherently more spiritual and religious than marriage. This has resulted in Rome's glorifying of celibacy, especially for her clergy.

The other reason is the Reformed emphasis upon marriage and family on account of the Reformed doctrine of the covenant. Since God establishes His covenant with believers and their children, gathering His church in the generations of believers and using the godly home to rear covenant children to maturity in Christ, the Reformed emphasis upon marriage is right. But such an emphasis on marriage which ignores or even disparages single life is wrong. Justice must be done to what I Corinthians 7 teaches about the single life. After all, this too is part of biblical doctrine. Besides, failure to reckon with the biblical teaching on single life discourages the unmarried. They begin to think of themselves as second-class citizens of the kingdom. Some may even plunge into a disastrous marriage in order to escape singleness. What is even worse, if we ignore what is said about single life for some, we hinder the life of special devotion to the Lord that some may very well choose to live as single.

Right in the middle of the outstanding passage on marriage, the Spirit of truth clearly and emphatically teaches that single life is honorable for some Christians.

A sketch of the passage will be helpful to show this. The background of chapter 7's teaching on marriage is the condemnation of fornication in chapter 6:9-20. Chapter 7:1a indicates the subject and approach of the chapter: answering questions on marriage matters. Verses 2-5 treat the sexual aspect of marriage. Verses 10-17 prohibit divorce and remarriage. Verses 18-24 contain the important reminder to all Christians that the earthly circumstances in which they find themselves — racial, social, economic, marital — become their calling from God. Believers are to accept these circumstances and live in them in the service of God. Verse 39 lays down the basic truth about marriage that governs everything that is said about marriage throughout the entire chapter.

This leaves two large sections of the chapter unaccounted for, verses 6-9 and verses 25-38. The subject in these passages is single life for Christians. And the very last word of the apostle in the great chapter on marriage is praise of single life: "But she (the widow) is happier if she so abide," that is, remains single (v. 40).

Singleness Is Honorable

Being single, being unmarried, is honorable for the Christian man and woman. Singleness as a lifelong state is honorable. In verses 1 and 8, the apostle states that being and remaining single is good for certain Christians: "It is good for a man not to touch a woman"; "It is good for (the unmarried and widows) if they abide even as I." The word translated "good" is the Greek word *kalos,* meaning "excellent" or "honorable," especially since the thing that is good is useful for worthwhile purposes.

In important respects, being single is preferable to marriage. According to verse 38 the father who marries off his daughter does well, but a father who keeps his daughter in single life does better. Verse 40 teaches that, although a widow may remarry, she is happier if she remains unmarried. This is not merely the personal opinion of Paul but the judgment of one who is conscious of having the Spirit of inspiration.

Indeed, the apostle could wish that all members of the congregation would remain single. He recommends this way of life, if a particular condition is met: "For I would that all men were even as I myself," that is, unmarried (v. 7a); "Art thou loosed from a wife? seek not a wife" (v. 27b).

The excellence of the single life is illustrated in Paul himself and was experienced by him. Paul was single, and he found single life rewarding, indeed much preferable to marriage.

The question is: In what does the goodness, or excellence, of single life for the Christian consist, and in what respect is it superior to marriage?

Single life is good inasmuch as marriage is not an absolute requirement for Christians. This is the apostle's point in verse 6: "But I speak this by permission, and not of commandment." He has just exhorted men and women in the church to marry and to live together sexually (vv. 2-5). Someone might suppose that this was a command to all without exception. Not so, says Paul in verse 6. To marry is permitted, not commanded. Therefore, single life is an option for the Christian. Singleness is an earthly way of life in which the believer may serve the Lord, as much as is marriage.

Single life is preferable to marriage because it allows one to devote himself or herself more fully to the Lord and to the work of the Lord. It is not the case that single life is preferable to marriage because marriage is inherently evil or because single life is intrinsically more spiritual and holy or because the single Christian merits salvation by remaining single.

But singleness can be useful to the kingdom of Christ. In certain instances it is very useful. Singleness lends itself to greater devotion and service to Christ. For single life is earthly life free from the cares and troubles of marriage. Paul has a strong awareness of the problems, burdens, and responsibilities of married life. He calls these responsibilities "the present distress" in verse 26 and "trouble in the flesh" in verse 28. The everyday pressure of these responsibilities upon the souls of married Christians and the demands of these responsibilities on their time, he describes as "carefulness" in verse 32: "I would have you without carefulness." The apostle recommends singleness because he wants to spare Christians these cares (v. 28).

But the purpose is not that the single Christian may be carefree, much less that he or she lead an irresponsible life. Rather, since the single life is free from the cares that invariably attend marriage, it can be devoted more fully to Christ. This is the teaching of verses 32ff. The unmarried person cares for the things of the Lord Jesus, how he may please the Lord. The married person cares for the things of the world — job, money, house, clothes, doctor bills, Christian school tuition, time for the family — how he may please wife and children. In this connection, the apostle advocates that fathers not give their virgin daughters in marriage; he wants these girls to attend upon the Lord without distraction (v. 35).

The single Christian can please the Lord in a special vocation. There is place, even need, for the unmarried pastor; the unmarried missionary; the unmarried teacher in the Christian school; the unmarried full-time assistant to the deacons (cf. I Tim. 5:9ff.).

The single Christian can please the Lord in an ordinary vocation. The single person has more time to pray; more time to study the Scriptures; more time to serve the other members of the church in their needs; more time and energy to volunteer for all kinds of tasks that promote the kingdom.

I say that single life can be devoted *more fully* to the Lord than married life because also Christian married life is devoted to the Lord. The apostle surely does not mean that the married believer is completely worldly, whereas the unmarried believer is completely otherworldly. Nevertheless, it is the case that the unmarried has time and energy that the married expends, and sometimes exhausts, upon the earthly cares of marriage and family.

Practical Implications for the Single

Important practical truths about singleness in the congregation and about the congregation's view of the singles follow from the apostle's teaching of the excellency of being unmarried.

First, it is wrong for the church to suppose that everyone ought to be married and that there is something shameful or doubtful about being unmarried. The married majority of the people of God may not look down on the "old maid" and "old batch." The opening and closing verses of one of the outstanding chapters in the Bible on marriage recommend their state.

Second, the unmarried themselves must not regard their singleness as failure and inferiority. Certainly, no one should plunge himself or herself into a foolish marriage, just to escape the "stigma" of being unmarried. Altogether apart from the apostle's spiritual outlook on single life, there is truth in Shakespeare's line, "Better well hanged than ill wed."

Third, some single young people, as well as the widows and widowers, may well ask themselves, "Am I possibly called by God to serve Him in singleness, and am I willing to do this?" There is still place in the Christian life for such devotion to Christ. There is still need in the kingdom for the work that such devotion performs.

But, fourth, the motivation must be spiritual: The single would devote himself or herself to Christ. For a young man to refuse marriage merely because he disliked the cares involved in marriage, having no intention to devote himself to Christ more fully, would not be honorable at all. The likelihood is that he will fall into the sin of fornication, or at least live the miserable life of always burning sexually.

This is I Corinthians 7's commendation and recommendation of single life.

If One Has the Gift

One condition qualifies everything that the apostle has to say about the advantages of single life: The man or woman must have the gift of self-control over the sexual desire — what Paul calls the ability to "contain" in verse 9. If one does not have this gift, he or she ought to marry. And since relatively few have this gift, the rule for Christians is that they marry. But if they are not able to be self-controlled sexually, let them marry! (v. 9) Even if one has this gift, he is free to marry. But if he lacks it, he ought to marry, lest he fall into fornication.

This leads naturally into the teaching of I Corinthians 7 concerning holy marriage. This is, in fact, the approach of the apostle: "Nevertheless, to avoid fornication, let every man have his own wife, and let every woman have her own husband" (I Cor. 7:2).

The Unwilling Single

Before we consider what the chapter teaches about marriage, a word is in order concerning a real problem with which some single Christians struggle. These are the singles who are unmarried not by choice and not because they have the special gift of being continent but because of the circumstances of their lives over which they have no control. They may desire marriage. They probably feel the need of marriage in what Paul calls "burning" in verse 9. But no one proposes marriage if they are women or no one accepts their proposal if they are men. Or there are other extraordinary circumstances that make marriage impossible for them.

What does Christ say to these believers?

First, "let them marry" (v. 9). Do they pray about their need? Do they ask a husband or a wife from the Sovereign of the universe? Are they being too choosy about a mate, even unbiblically choosy? Is the main criterion for the man that the woman be beautiful rather than that she fear the Lord? Does the young woman turn down and turn away the young men of the church who are not handsome and dashing suitors according to the standards of the romance magazines of the world? Are both the young men and the young women waiting for the feeling of falling madly in love, when they have every right to proceed with marriage on the basis of their unity in Christ, their suitability for each other, and their warm affection for each other?

It is the duty of the young men of the church to date and marry the daughters of the church, and it is the calling of the young women to accept the young men.

This is implied in the command of verse 39, "(Marry) in the Lord."

Still, God makes marriage impossible for some. These Christians are to accept the single life submissively as the will of God for them. They should learn to view their single life not simply as a cross to bear but as the specific way of life in which they are to glorify God. Are they called being single? Let them not trouble themselves about these circumstances of their earthly life but serve God in these circumstances. Let them seize singleness as the opportunity to serve the Lord Christ more fully than would be possible if they were married. They may trust that God's grace will be sufficient, particularly for sexual self-control. They are required to abstain from sexual relationships, that is, from fornication. This is possible. Jesus taught that some make themselves eunuchs for the kingdom's sake (Matt. 19:12). Not only is there the gift of sexual self-control, but there is also the powerful grace of self-discipline and chastity.

Chapter 4
Bound for Life

The wife is bound by the law as long as her husband liveth; but if her husband be dead, she is at liberty to be married to whom she will; only in the Lord.
— *I Corinthians 7:39*

Single life is perfectly honorable. Ordinarily, however, God both calls us to marriage and opens up the way for us to be married. The rule for Christians is marriage: "If they cannot contain, let them marry" (v. 9). It is better to marry. To the teaching of I Corinthians 7 on marriage, we now turn.

What marriage is, the Holy Spirit tells us in verse 39: "The wife is bound by the law as long as her husband liveth; but if her husband be dead, she is at liberty to be married to whom she will; only in the Lord." The apostle of Christ indicates the essence of marriage also in verse 27: "Art thou bound unto a wife? seek not to be loosed."

Lifelong Bond

Marriage is a lifelong bond between one woman and one man, formed by God the Creator who created man and woman for marriage and marriage for man and woman. Marriage is not a human contract dependent on the two parties fulfilling the agreed-upon stipulations, although there certainly are mutual duties in marriage.

Neither is marriage a conditional promise that the husband and wife make to each other, although they do enter upon marriage by way of a solemn promise. But marriage is a bond that joins the two. It is a union and communion.

It is a special bond, indeed a unique bond. There are other bonds, e.g., that of parent and child and that of two friends. But there is none like the bond of marriage. This is the only one-flesh bond. This is the only bond to which belongs the sexual relationship. But it is a bond. "The wife is *bound*," according to verse 39, that is, she is bound to her husband. The sense is that the wife is bonded to her husband.

Because marriage is essentially a bond of love and friendship between the two, it serves as the earthly symbol of the covenant-relation between God and His people. In the age of the old covenant, the prophets described the special relationship between Jehovah and Israel as marriage (cf. Ezek. 16). Ezekiel 16:8 explicitly identifies marriage as "covenant" (cf. Mal. 2:14). The fulfillment of the covenant in Jesus Christ is the marriage of Christ and the church according to the apostle in Ephesians 5:22ff.[13]

The bond that constitutes earthly marriage is made by God. I Corinthians 7:39 literally reads, "the wife *has been* bound." She did not bind herself to the man she married. Neither did her husband bind her to himself. No earthly agency at all binds two married persons, whether state, or church, or parents. But God binds wife and husband. The "law" spoken of in verse 39 as the

---

[13]   For a development of a doctrine of marriage as an unbreakable bond that symbolizes the marriage covenant between Christ and His church, see my *Marriage: The Mystery of Christ and the Church* (Grand Rapids, MI: Reformed Free Publishing Association, 1975, reprint 1983).

instrument by which the wife has been bound to her husband is the living Word of God functioning in the realm of creation.

Whenever a man and a woman willingly engage to marry, have the union sanctioned by a proper authority, and consummate the relationship sexually, God binds them in His institution of marriage. In the words "has been bound" in verse 39, the apostle expresses what we read about marriage in the creation account in Genesis 2:18ff. and what Jesus teaches about marriage in Matthew 19:4-6, namely, that God has joined husband and wife together in the one-flesh bond.

The bond is for life: "as long as her husband liveth." The Holy Spirit could not make the truth of marriage simpler or clearer than He does here. The church has always understood this truth very well. For a thousand years after the time of the apostles, it was the virtually unanimous judgment of the church that marriage was for life so that all remarriage during the life of the original mate was forbidden, even when divorce had taken place on the ground of adultery. Until recent times, the marriage form universally used in "church weddings" required that the persons marrying promise to take each other as husband and wife "until death us do part." Still today, when churches and theologians accept and justify divorce and remarriage for many reasons, even those writers who maintain that marriage can be dissolved apart from death and who sanction remarriage while an original mate is yet living grudgingly admit that the idea and ideal of marriage are that it be lifelong.

Loosing

Since wife and husband are bound and since it is God

who has done the binding, the only loosing is that which is done by God, namely, the death of one of the married persons. As plainly as language can state it is it taught by the Holy Spirit in verse 39 that death, and only death, dissolves the marriage bond: "but if her husband be dead, she is at liberty to be married to whom she will...."

It is a mistake, therefore, to explain I Corinthians 7:27, 28 as permitting a divorced Christian to remarry. In this passage the apostle does indeed permit the man who has been "loosed" from his wife to marry again: "Art thou bound unto a wife? seek not to be loosed. Art thou loosed from a wife? seek not a wife. But and if thou marry, thou hast not sinned...."

But a divorced man has not been loosed from his wife. He is divorced but not loosed. For I Corinthians 7:39 makes plain that the only loosing of a wife from her husband, or of a husband from his wife, is death. The divorced man is still bound to a wife. He may not seek another wife.

That man who has been loosed from a wife so that he does not sin if he marries again is the man whose wife has died. The reference of I Corinthians 7:27, 28 is to the widower.

The Practice of the Bond

This fundamental truth of the lifelong bond governs everything that Paul teaches about marriage in I Corinthians 7. This is the principle that controls Christian marriage practice.

Fornication is forbidden and sex within marriage is commanded as a duty because sexual intimacy is a vital part of the bond.

Separation and divorce are forbidden because they tear at the bond.

The wife may not marry another man while her husband is living because this violently violates the bond.

Whatever has to do with marriage, sexual ethics, separation, divorce, remarriage, and family must reckon with this foundation-truth and reality: Marriage is a lifelong bond formed by God. Christian marriage lives or dies in a church as this principle is maintained or abandoned. To paraphrase Luther, it is the article of the standing or falling of the church with regard to marriage, sexual holiness, and the home.

The sorry fact is that many churches have fallen!

We must take note of the apostle's application of this fundamental truth of marriage to several practical aspects of marriage.

First, the marriage sanctioned by God and alone approved by the obedient church is the monogamous bond between one man and one woman. Each man is to have his own wife, and each woman is to have her own husband (v. 2). Plurality of wives or of husbands is condemned, whether this plurality be simultaneous or successive. There may be no homosexual pseudo-marriage.

Second, life and conduct within marriage ought to be characterized by mutuality. Husband and wife share in every aspect of married life, together engage in behavior of mutual giving and receiving, actively participate in one life of communion. This is the heart and secret of marriage. Granted, this does not rule out order in the marriage. Ephesians 5:22-33 teaches that the husband enters into the communion of marriage as the head who has authority and that the wife enters into the communion of marriage as the body who willingly is submissive. But this order does not exclude, overshadow, or weaken the friendship, the mutuality, of the marriage. For marriage is a bond.

Mutuality is a striking feature of the practice of Christian marriage in I Corinthians 7. To avoid fornication, every man has his own wife, but every woman also has her own husband (v. 2). The husband pays off his sexual debt to his wife, but also the wife pays off her debt to her husband (v. 3). The wife does not have sole authority over her body, but neither does the husband have authority over his body (v. 4). If there is abstinence from sexual relations, it is by mutual consent (v. 5). The wife may not leave her husband, but neither may the husband divorce his wife (vv. 10,11). Unbelieving husbands are sanctified by believing wives, but so are unbelieving wives sanctified by believing husbands (vv. 12-14.). Wives must care for the things of everyday life, how they may please their husbands, but husbands must do the very same (vv. 33, 34).

The apostle is perfectly even-handed as regards behavior in marriage. This is not because he is temporarily delivered from his male chauvinism, but because he knows marriage to be the most intimate bond of friendship.

If believing husbands and wives will practice this mutuality from the first day of their marriage, peace and bliss are assured. Failure here will result in misery, if not marital disaster.

A third practical application of the basic truth that marriage is a lifelong bond is that every believer is called to marry "in the Lord (Jesus)" (v. 39). The believer may marry only a person with whom he or she is one in Christ, one in the truth of the Holy Scriptures, and one in church membership.

The marriage of a believer and an unbeliever is a valid marriage, a real marriage, as is the marriage of two unbelievers. The validity of the marriage of believer and unbeliever is insisted on in verses 12-16: If a brother has an unbelieving wife, let him not put her away; if a sister has an unbelieving husband, let her not leave him. They are truly married. Marriage is not a church ordinance like the sacraments but a creation ordinance like civil government. So wonderfully tight is the bond and so does God wonderfully protect His saint in the bond that the marriage of a believer and an unbeliever is not polluted by the unbeliever but sanctified by the believer. Also, the children of the mixed marriage are holy, covenant children: "Else were your children unclean; but now are they holy" (v. 14).

Even so, what a lack, at best, of the most precious oneness of all, and, at worst, what disharmony. What must it be to live in marriage with someone who rejects Jesus Christ as Lord and Savior!

Young people, widows, widowers, all unmarried Christians, if they marry, must marry in the Lord.

Marriage as Calling

Fourth, living married life rightly is, for every married Christian, a calling from God. God has bound married Christians, and He privileges and requires them to glorify Him by honorable behavior in the bond. The single, most important, absolutely decisive question for the married Christian is not "Am I happy?" or "Am I fulfilled?" or "Do I feel that I love my husband or wife any longer?" or "Is my wife or husband keeping her or his end of the bargain (as though marriage were a bargain!)?" But the question is just this, come what may: "Will I or will I not walk as God has distributed to me in my marriage and as the Lord has called me in my marriage?" (cf. v. 17) Marriage is holy not only because the institution is good and sleeping together is pure but

also, and especially, because marriage is consecrated to
God.

Living rightly in marriage is not easy. The Bible
never says that it is. On the contrary, the Bible warns
believers that every marriage, every marriage *of those
who marry in the Lord,* will have its share of troubles.
Those who marry will have "trouble in the flesh" (v. 28).
They will have cares (v. 32). Is there any marriage that
has never been strained by these troubles that must
come when two sinful people are bound as closely as is
the case in marriage? Is there any marriage that has not
been oppressed by the burden of the special responsibilities that come with marriage, particularly when the
marriage produces children who also are sinful?

Martin Luther begins his commentary on I
Corinthians 7 by freely acknowledging the folly of
marrying on account of the earthly troubles:

> "What a fool is he who takes a wife," says the
> world, and it is certainly true. And many learned
> scholars have decided that a wise man should not
> take a wife, even if she were wisdom personified.
> This, too, is true and well said, for those who
> believe that there is no life after this one (as such
> people do) act almost wisely in falling back on free
> fornication and not tying themselves to the labor
> of married life. In this way they have at least fewer
> evil days in this life.

He immediately adds:

> But on the other hand the Spirit says: "He is a wise
> man who takes a wife." This, too, is certainly true,
> and this truth leads to the conclusion that a wise
> man should take a wife, even though she were
> foolishness personified. This, too, is right and well
> said, for since a Christian man is waiting for

another life after this one, it is a matter of wisdom
that he should have fewer good days on earth so
that in eternal life he might enjoy only happy
ones.[14]

Then Luther married and discovered that there was
a great deal more happiness in marriage than he supposed in 1523.

The traditional Dutch Reformed marriage form is
biblical, realistic, and helpful when it begins, "Whereas
married persons are generally, by reason of sin, subject
to many troubles and afflictions, to the end that you ...
may also be assured in your hearts of the certain assis-
tance of God in your afflictions, hear therefore from the
Word of God how honorable the marriage state is ...."

How wonderful, in this connection, is the wisdom of
Reformed churches today. The troubles and afflictions
of married persons due to sin are wreaking havoc upon
marriages in their fellowship as never before in history.
And just at this time they jettison the old marriage form
as "too gloomy" and adopt a new form that presents
marriage as a bed of roses.

The story is told of the pious, old Dutch wife who
was asked by friends at the celebration of her fiftieth
wedding anniversary, "*Vrouw*, in all those years did you
ever contemplate divorce?" After a long moment's
reflection, she replied thoughtfully, "No, not divorce.
Murder, a couple of times, but never divorce."

Married persons are generally by reason of sin subject to many troubles. In the times of trouble, the sense
of calling sees the believers through. The reason why

---

[14]   Hilton C. Oswald, ed., *Luther's Works*, Volume 28 (Saint Louis:
Concordia Publishing House, 1973), p. 5.

there are many more divorces in the churches today than there were 50 years ago is not that the troubles have increased but that the sense of calling has decreased. Thus is fulfilled the prophecy of Christ when He said, "When the Son of man cometh, shall he find faith on the earth?" (Luke 18:8).

Living as Though Unmarried

Although a calling and although of the greatest importance for the present existence of the kingdom of Christ, marriage is not of ultimate importance. This is the final practical application of the basic truth about marriage that the apostle makes in I Corinthians 7. All must "sit loose to their marriage," so to speak: "They that have wives (must) be as though they had none" (v. 29). For the time has been shortened, the time both of the life of each married person and the time of history itself. The form of this world is passing away. The bond of marriage is lifelong, but only lifelong. God will surely loose the bond by the death of one of the married persons. He will abolish the institution itself at the coming of Christ (cf. Matt. 22:30).

Does someone have a bad marriage? Let this encourage her. Is someone in danger of making an idol out of his marriage? Let this warn him. Does someone suffer because God withholds marriage from her? Let this comfort her.

The earthly symbol is quickly, finally, and utterly dissolved. Only the heavenly reality lasts forever: the bond of love and friendship, the covenant bond, the mystical union, that unites every believer with Jesus Christ.

Upon this, the real marriage, unmarried and married alike are to set their hearts.

Chapter 5
Let Them Not Divorce

Let not the wife depart from her husband ...
and let not the husband put away his wife.
— *I Corinthians 7:10, 11*

The questions raised by the subject of this chapter put us to the test, whether we meant what we confessed about sex and marriage, on the basis of the apostle's teaching in I Corinthians 7, in the preceding chapters. These are such questions as "May Christians desert their mates?" "May Christians ever divorce?" "If Christians divorce, may they remarry?" "Is remarriage ever permitted for Christians?"

These questions confront not only the individual believer but also the church. What must the church's stand be on these vital issues? What must be her teaching as she carries out that aspect of the "great commission" of Matthew 28:18-20 that is often overlooked and sorely neglected: "Teaching them to observe all things whatsoever I have commanded you"? What must be her discipline as she works to bring the erring and disobedient to repentance, thus keeping the congregation pure from the leaven of unfaithfulness and adultery and thus honoring the name of her faithful, covenant God? Much depends upon the church's stand since the instituted church is the pillar and ground of the truth of marriage and family, as she is the pillar and ground of all truth (I Tim. 3:15).

In light of the clear teaching of the apostle of Christ in I Corinthians 7 concerning the essence of marriage, considered in the preceding chapter, it is not difficult to answer these questions about desertion, divorce, and remarriage. It is sometimes painful to answer them, but it is not difficult.

If marriage is a lifelong bond formed by God Himself between one man and one woman, as the apostle teaches in verse 39, desertion, divorce, and remarriage are forbidden to Christians and are outlawed from the church. Desertion and divorce are also ruled out by the teaching in verses 2-5 that sex is a debt owed by the husband to his wife and by the wife to her husband, for desertion and divorce are non-payment of the debt. Remarriage is prohibited by the teaching of the apostle in chapter 6:13-20 and in chapter 7:2, 5 that a sexual relationship with any other beside one's wife or husband is fornication, since remarriage while the original mate is still living does establish a sexual relationship with another.

Pious Talk

But did we mean what we said about the marriage relation's being a permanent bond and what we said about sex outside the bond being fornication? Or was that merely pious talk? There is a great deal of pious talk today about marriage and about the family both on the part of theologians and on the part of the instituted church. In their speeches and writings or in their synodical reports, they carry on at great length, saying the nicest things about marriage and the family — how important the family is, that marriage is ideally for life, and that marriage must be defended and promoted by believers and church.

The bottom line or last page, however, is that Christians are allowed to forsake and divorce their wives or husbands for more than one reason, if not for any reason, and to remarry. Not only the "innocent party" but also the guilty party in the breakup of the marriage is permitted to remarry. All may consider themselves good Christians. All may remain members in good standing in the congregation including those who have remarried each other's husbands or wives. All may come to the table of the Lord.

In the opening chapters of his book *Marriage, Divorce & Remarriage in the Bible*,[15] Jay E. Adams has good things to say about marriage as an institution of God, including that it is "a formal (covenantal) arrangement between two persons to become each other's loving companions for life" (p. 13). In the concluding chapters, however, he tells us that "remarriage (after divorce — DJE), in general, is not only allowed but in some cases encouraged and commanded. It is looked upon favorably in the NT" (p. 86). Adams approves the remarriage of the guilty party as well as of the "innocent party" in a divorce and indeed of all who unbiblically divorce their mates. The counsel of Adams to those seeking to know the will of God concerning marriage and remarriage is that "remarriage, in general, is desirable" (p. 97). This is the book on marriage, divorce, and remarriage that conservatives recommend!

The guidelines in matters of marriage, divorce, and remarriage adopted by the Christian Reformed Church in 1980 are typical of the public pronouncements on these matters by Reformed and Presbyterian churches in reaction to the appalling number of divorces and

---

15   Grand Rapids, MI: Baker Book House, 1980.

remarriages in these churches. They begin well, very well, creating hope that finally a Reformed church will take a stand on the basis of the Word of God against the wicked, destructive, scandalous attack on the funda-mental ordinance of marriage and family in our day.

> The church has a special interest in marriage and the family, for the Christian family is an important witness to the unity Christ creates.... Instruction is especially important in an age when the Christian view of marriage is not understood and often under attack. Therefore, the church must pro-claim and teach the biblical doctrine of marriage.... To achieve this, the church must: ... Stress the God-willed permanence of marriage and counsel against violation of the marriage bond.... The permanence of the marriage relationship lies at the heart of the biblical teaching on marriage. God wills a lifelong unity of husband and wife in marriage. Conse-quently, the basic declaration of Scripture is that divorce and remarriage while one's spouse is alive constitutes adultery.

But the hope that the church will have the courage of these convictions, that is, that she means what she says by these fine words, is soon dashed. For at once the guidelines go on to affirm the right of the married person whose mate has been guilty of "unchastity" to remarry. They then venture the judgment that the Scriptures do not clearly forbid other remarriages. The conclusion is:

> The church should neither issue a clear prohibi-tion of remarriage in those cases where Scripture is unclear, nor should it attempt to list with legal precision the circumstances under which any par-ticular remarriage does not conflict with biblical teaching.... Therefore, the church must ... deal pastorally with those who have failed to keep the

> biblical principle by ... refraining from a strictly
> legal approach to remarriage that tries to provide
> a basis for judgment that certain categories of
> remarriage are always compatible or incompat-
> ible with the teachings of Scripture.[16]

The effect of the policy set forth in the guidelines, despite their clear recognition and confession of the life-long, permanent nature of the marriage bond, is to throw the door of the church wide open to divorces and remarriages for every reason. The door of heaven will not be thrown open as wide.

Yet one more instance of the "pious talk" about marriage is the article on the "Theology of Marriage" in the recently published *Encyclopedia of the Reformed Faith*.[17] Shirley C. Guthrie opens beautifully: "Reformed Christians have typically agreed that marriage is a life partnership analogous to the covenant relationship between God and God's people in Scripture." She ends miserably:

> Most Reformed Christians today acknowledge
> that divorce can be the legitimate recognition that
> human error and/or sin may prevent a marriage
> from becoming a true life partnership. When a
> marriage ends in divorce — as when it begins and
> continues — Christians count on the grace of God
> that both forgives sinful people and enables them
> to make fresh starts (including the possibility of
> new marriage for divorced persons) (pp. 235, 236).

As the ministers and synods engage in this pious

---

[16]   Quoted in *Manual of Christian Reformed Church Government (1980)*, William P. Brink and Richard R. De Ridder (Grand Rapids, MI: Board of Publications of the Christian Reformed Church, 1980), pp. 269-274.

[17]   Donald K. McKim, ed. (Louisville, Kentucky: John Knox Press, 1992).

talk, the tidal wave of abandonment, divorce, and remarriage rolls over their congregations so that by their
own admission the rate of divorce and remarriage in
evangelical churches in the United States is exactly that
in the world about them.

The Uncompromising Word of Christ

The apostle of Christ is not guilty of pious talk in I
Corinthians 7. Uncompromisingly, he applies the truth
about marriage and the truth about sex to the issues of
desertion, divorce, and remarriage. These were press-
ing problems to some Christians at Corinth even as they
are to some Christians today. Among the questions on
marriage matters that the Corinthians put to the apostle
according to verse 1 were questions concerning leaving
their mates and remarrying. Paul answers these questions in verses 10-17. But he does not answer these
questions by contradicting or undermining everything
that he has taught about sex and marriage in the preceding verses or by negating what he will teach about the
essential nature of marriage as a lifelong bond in verse
39.

What the apostle teaches about desertion, divorce,
and remarriage is authoritative for all Christians and all
churches in all times and places. He prefaces his instruction on these matters with the words, "And unto the
married I command ..." (v. 10). Indeed, what he says to
married Christians about desertion, divorce, and remarriage in verses 10 and 11 is not his own command
but the command of Jesus Christ Himself who is, Paul
reminds us, the Lord of church and Christian: "... yet not
I, but the Lord" (v. 10).

Nor is the authoritative character of the instruction
weakened in verse 12, where the apostle says that with

regard to what follows it is not the Lord but Paul who speaks. In verses 12ff., Paul gives command concerning mixed marriages, the marriages of believers with unbelievers. Jesus had not addressed this situation during His earthly ministry. Therefore, Paul cannot appeal to any teaching of Jesus now recorded in the gospels as he could in the matter of the divorcing and remarrying of two who belong to the covenant community.

But what Paul himself teaches is fully as binding as that which Jesus taught and which the apostle merely quotes. For Paul is Christ's commissioned apostle whose word is inspired. At the end of all this practical teaching on marriage, Paul says, "I think also that I have the Spirit of God" (v. 40). At the end of this particular section, in which he treats desertion, divorce, and remarriage, he says, "And so ordain I in all churches" (v. 17).

The instruction on desertion, divorce, and remarriage in I Corinthians 7:10-17 is apostolic command and ordinance and, therefore, the rule for all churches and for all Christians until the world's end.

The question for churches and Christians at the end of the twentieth century is simply this, "Will we obey the Word of Christ as written by His apostle or not?" "Is Christ or culture going to determine our doctrine and practice in the vital area of the Christian life that consists of fidelity in marriage?" Culture, that is, the ungodly world, has decided marriage-doctrine and marriage-practice for much of the nominally Christian church and for many professing Christians in our day. The result is scandal, confusion, and woe. For the faithful church and for the true believer, Christ rules in the matters of desertion, divorce, and remarriage. He rules by the Holy Scriptures, His Word. He rules by His Word in I Corinthians 7:10-17.

The Forbidding of Divorce

The Lord commands all married Christians not to desert, put away, or divorce their husbands or wives. In verses 10 and 11, He applies this prohibition to married believers whose husbands or wives are also Christians and members of the church.

> And unto the married I command, yet not I, but the Lord, Let not the wife depart from her husband:
> But and if she depart, let her remain unmarried, or be reconciled to her husband: and let not the husband put away his wife.

The wife may not depart; the husband may not put away. This refers to every form of separation, or breakup, of the two, whether simple separation, legal separation, or full, legal divorce. Marriage is a one-flesh bond requiring that the two dwell together as the apostle expresses it in verses 12 and 13. Literally, he speaks of their "housing with each other." Marriage is a bond of bed and board. Therefore, every such kind of physical separation is violation of the deepest nature of marriage.

This is Christ's command even though He knows very well the trouble, the distress, that this may mean for some Christians. As the promise of "trouble in the flesh" in verse 28 and the mention of the apostle's desire that the saints be "without carefulness" (literally: "free from cares") in verse 32 make plain, the Scriptures have a realistic view of the marriages of Christians. Every marriage has its burdens and hardships. For some Christians the burdens are especially heavy and the hardships are especially severe. There are harsh, tyrannical husbands in the church. To live with these men is miserable for the wife. There are also women who are described in Proverbs as brawling and contentious so that the poor husbands feel that they rather dwell in the wilderness alone than to live with these wives (cf. Proverbs 21:9, 19; 25:24; 27:15).

"Let not the wife depart!" "Let not the husband put away!"   Marriage is living together until death, "for better, for worse."

This does not imply that Christ or His church simply preaches to the married in the congregation, "Do not separate," and nothing more. In Ephesians 5:22-33, the Word beseeches wives to live with their husbands as the church lives with Christ, that is, in the obedience of love, and husbands to live with their wives as Christ lives with the church, that is, in the headship of love. In I Corinthians 7:33, 34, Christian husbands and wives are taught that they must make it their goal to please each other.

> But he that is married careth for the things that are of the world, how he may please his wife.
> There is difference also between a wife and a virgin. The unmarried woman careth for the things of the Lord, that she may be holy both in body and in spirit: but she that is married careth for the things of the world, how she may please her husband.

The marriages of Christians need not be miserable on account of the harshness of husbands or the nagging of wives. The marriages of Christians *may* not be miserable for these reasons. It is sin for a husband to be a brute or for a wife to be a shrew. But even if a marriage is bedeviled by trouble of this kind, separation or divorce is not the solution to the problem.

The Mixed Marriage

How insistent and comprehensive this prohibition against separation really is comes out when the apostle applies it to Christians married to unbelievers. This, he does in verses 12 and 13:

> ... If any brother hath a wife that believeth not, and she be pleased to dwell with him, let him not put her away.
> And the woman which hath an husband that believeth not, and if he be pleased to dwell with her, let her not leave him.

Paul addresses believers in a mixed marriage. The explanation for the mixed marriage is not that these believers had disobeyed the injunction expressed in verse 39 that believers marry only in the Lord. Rather, they had married when both they and their mates were in their original paganism. Then the gospel came, and only they were converted. Their mates were left in unbelief. Now these Christians found themselves in the most miserable marriage situation of all: Yoked together with unbelievers. Righteousness and unrighteousness, light and darkness, Christ and Belial, the temple of God and an idol shared bed and board. It is no wonder that they anxiously asked their apostle whether they should separate. Their motive was the fear that the very close fellowship of marriage would pollute them, the believers, thus destroying them spiritually and eternally.

Commands the apostle, "Let not the wife leave the unbelieving husband!" "Let not the husband put away the unbelieving wife!" There may be no separation, not even in this, the most difficult, strained, distressing, trouble-filled marriage of all. For the two are validly married. God has bound them in the one-flesh union. Marriage is a creation ordinance, not a sacrament. And married persons must honor the ordinance of God by living with each other.

Obedience to this command is motivated in several respects. First, the believer may trust that God will work upon the marriage in a special way so that the relationship itself will be sanctified by the holiness of the believer rather than being corrupted by the unholiness of the unbeliever. This is what is meant in verse 14 by the unbeliever's being sanctified by his believing wife or by her believing husband. The reference is not to a spiritual cleansing of the heart for in the case under consideration the sanctified husband or wife is and remains an unbeliever. But the unbeliever is sanctified as regards her or his position in the marriage relationship so that the believer will not be corrupted even though she or he constantly "touch(es) ... the unclean" (II Cor. 6:17). This is an extraordinary operation of the Holy Spirit, and one that indicates how important it is to God that His people maintain even the most difficult marriage, for every other friendship of believer and unbeliever corrupts the believer.

A second motivation of the believer for maintaining a mixed marriage is that his or her godly conduct in the marriage may be a means to save the unbeliever. This is held out to the believer in verse 16: "For what knowest thou, O wife, whether thou shalt save thy husband? or how knowest thou, O man, whether thou shalt save thy wife?" Peter encourages believing women with unbelieving husbands similarly in I Peter 3:1, 2, calling attention to the power of the wives' behavior in the winning of their unconverted husbands.

Likewise, ye wives, be in subjection to your

own husbands; that, if any obey not the word, they
also may without the word be won by the conver-
sation of the wives;
    While they behold your chaste conversation
coupled with fear.

In an environment controlled by the holiness of the
believer, when that relationship is involved which God
Himself wills to honor, and where children are found
whom the Word calls holy, it is a real possibility that
God will work regeneration in the unbelieving marriage partner. Then there is a personal sanctification
where formerly there was merely positional sanctification.

It is noteworthy that, as regards the decision to live
with the unbeliever or to separate from him, the believer
must be motivated by consideration of the welfare of the
other, not by consideration of her own interests. The
question is not "What would be easier and more pleas-
ant for you?" But the question is "What knowest thou,
O wife, whether thou shalt save thy husband?" This is
the uniquely Christian viewpoint: Self is sacrificed to
the love of the neighbor for God's sake.

Covenant Children

The third motivation is the children produced by the
mixed marriage: "... else were your children unclean;
but now are they holy" (v. 14b). Like the children of two
believing parents, the children of only one believing
parent are holy, covenant children, although not apart
from the believer's baptizing them and rearing them in
the fear of the Lord. This is a powerful proof in the New
Testament for the doctrine of the inclusion of the children of believers in the new covenant and infant baptism. The children of a believer, as children, as children

newly born, are cleansed from sin and consecrated to God. Possessing the reality, namely, renewal by the Holy Spirit, they may not be denied the sign, namely, baptism. Clearly implied is the truth of the covenant, that God is pleased to gather His church in the line of the generations of believers.

The argument against this explanation of the apostle's description of the children of the believer as holy by the opponents of the covenant and infant baptism has some appearance of soundness. The anti-covenantal argument is that just as the first part of verse 14 speaks of a holiness of the unbelieving wife or husband that has to do merely with external position and that certainly does not require baptism, so also with regard to the holiness of the children mentioned in the latter part of the verse. But this argument fails to observe that the assertion of the holiness of the children functions in the text as the basis of the declaration that in a mixed marriage the unbeliever is sanctified by the believer. If the apostle had written "The unbeliever is sanctified by his believing wife *and* your children are holy," the argument that in both instances holiness refers merely to outward position would hold. But in fact the apostle wrote, "The unbeliever is sanctified by the believer, *as is evident from the holiness of the children produced by this union.*" If the holiness of the children is merely the same as that of the unbelieving parent, the holiness of the children cannot serve as the ground for the declaration that the unbelieving parent is sanctified. Only if the holiness of the children is genuine, covenantal holiness consisting of fellowship with God by the inward work of the Spirit of Christ, does it prove that the marriage relationship of believer and unbeliever is controlled by the holiness of the believer.

The children of only one believing parent are born

again and holy. No more than in the case of the children of two believing parents is this true of every child. When the Scriptures speak of the saved children of believers, it has the elect children in view (cf. Rom. 9:6ff.). Nor is it true of all elect children without exception that they are regenerated and sanctified in childhood. But this is the rule according to the Scriptures, as is implied by the fifth commandment of the law and as is indicated by the examples of Jacob and John the Baptist when yet in their mothers' wombs (cf. Gen. 25:21-26; Luke 1:15, 41, 44).

In this way there is brought into the treatment of marriage in I Corinthians 7 one of the most important purposes of God with the marriages of His people. Usually, God wills the bringing forth of children who are members of His church by His covenant mercy.

But this is additional reason why the believing parent should stay in a difficult marriage and make the best of it. A strong motivation should be the welfare of the children. Desertion and divorce are destructive of the children. Even the world laments this evil. School psychologists tell us that the main mental health problem of school-age children is the turmoil of living through the divorce of their parents.

Allan Bloom has written that divorce is "surely America's most urgent social problem" because of the devastating effects that divorce has upon the children.

Bloom decries the deleterious effect that divorce has on university students. "When these students arrive at the university, they are not only reeling from the destructive effects of the overturning of faith and the ambiguity of loyalty that result from divorce, but deafened by self-serving lies and hypocrisies expressed in a pseudoscientific jargon." The "pseudoscientific jargon" is the glib talk of the psychologists brought in by the divorcing parents to justify the divorce to the children. In a remarkable passage, Bloom, an unbeliever, writes:

> The important lesson that the family taught was the existence of the only unbreakable bond, for better or for worse, between human beings. The decomposition of this bond is surely America's most urgent social problem. But nobody even tries to do anything about it. The tide seems to be irresistible. Among the many items on the agenda of those promoting America's moral regeneration, I never find marriage and divorce.[18]

This man from the University of Chicago shall rise up in the judgment with this generation of evangelicals and "conservatives" and shall condemn it.

Members in the churches opened wide to divorce and remarriage do sometimes cry out for deliverance from their misery by reformation of the churches' doctrine and practice of marriage. I have never forgotten the haunting (anonymous) article that appeared in the religious periodical *The Banner* under the title "Where Are We? Where Are We Going?" It was the cry of a broken heart. It pleaded with the church fathers to

> take a firm and decided stand against divorce.... Convince me, if you can, that those who, in the name of love, smash to bits the happinesses of father, mother, sister, brother, child, pastor, and church are keeping the law of love! Convince me that a denomination which baptizes such actions by silence or by a subdued reprimand is acting out of love![19]

---

[18]   *The Closing of the American Mind* (New York: Simon and Schuster, 1987), pp. 118-121.

[19]   "Where are We? Where are We Going?," *The Banner* 112, no. 47 (December 9, 1977), pp. 18, 19.

In Malachi 2:11-16, the prophet inveighs against the evil of divorce in Judah. The attitude of Jehovah God toward divorce is that He "hateth putting away." The people of the covenant are reminded that in the beginning God made the man and the woman one in marriage. And the reason was that "He might seek a godly seed." For the sake of a godly seed among our children, we may not desert or divorce.

If natural love for one's physical offspring ought to move a man or a woman to endure an "unhappy marriage," how much more, love for children who are not only one's own flesh and blood but also dear children of God by virtue of His covenant. Desertion and divorce of their wives or husbands by professing Christians when the marriage has produced children is the modern form of the practice of Old Testament Israel of offering God's children to Molech (cf. Lev. 18:21; II Kings 23:10; Jer. 32:35; Ezek. 16:21).

One of the most vehement condemnations in all of the Scriptures is reserved for husbands and wives who abandon their families, thus neglecting to supply the basic physical needs of wife or husband and of children. "But if any provide not for his own, and specially for those of his own house, he hath denied the faith, and is worse than an infidel" (I Tim. 5:8).

The forbidding of divorce even in the case of a mixed marriage and the demand that believers maintain even this, the most difficult of marriages, indicate the strength of the biblical prohibition against desertion and divorce and the rigor of the biblical insistence that believers maintain their marriages.

The contempt for God's hatred of divorce by the multitudes of professing Christians who desert and divorce and the churches' tolerance of divorce in the face of the express prohibition of desertion and divorce in I

Corinthians 7 plainly show that the religion of these
people and churches is not the Christianity of the apostle
of Christ.

When Separation Is Permitted

There is an exception to the prohibition against a
wife's leaving her husband. Having said, "Let not the
wife depart" in verse 10, the apostle immediately adds,
"But and if she depart." He then goes on to instruct the
departing wife as to her calling in this case. There is a
lawful separation from her husband by a Christian wife.
There is a separation that God does not condemn and
that the church may not censure.

Separation is not the rule. The rule is "No separation!" Separation is an exception. It is always a rare
thing in the church.

Nevertheless, separation is a possibility. Wives are
sometimes permitted to leave their husbands: "But and
if she depart ...."

The reason for the lawful separation is clearly implied in the apostle's words in verses 10 and 11. Paul
tells us that he is here only repeating the command of the
Lord Jesus concerning divorce: "I command, yet not I,
but the Lord." When the Lord gave command concerning divorce in Matthew 5:31, 32, Matthew 19:3-12, and
Mark 10:2-12, the one exception to His prohibition
against divorce was the fornication of one's mate.

> It hath been said, Whosoever shall put away
> his wife, let him give her a writing of divorcement:
> But I say unto you, That whosoever shall put
> away his wife, saving for the cause of fornication,
> causeth her to commit adultery: and whosoever
> shall marry her that is divorced committeth adul-
> tery (Matt. 5:31, 32).

Fornication, in Jesus' teaching, was the one ground for separation or divorce. Since Paul is reminding believers of Jesus' own teaching on divorce, the possibility of the wife's leaving her husband must be that permitted by Jesus, namely, her husband's sexual relationship with another than herself.

It is implied in verse 11 that it is also permissible under certain circumstances for the husband to put away his wife. The circumstances are the fornication of his wife.

Whether a temporary or even legal separation, in distinction from a legal divorce, is ever permitted a Christian for some reason other than the sexual sin of her husband or his wife is a difficult question. The Scriptures give no other ground for leaving or putting away than fornication. The weight of Scripture's teaching on marriage falls on calling the believer to live with her husband or his wife even though doing so means suffering. In such a case, wife or husband should accept the difficult marriage with all its difficulties as a calling from the Lord, bearing the suffering for the sake of Christ. The word of the apostle in verse 29 is encouragement to wives with a husband like Nabal and to husbands who must dwell with brawling women: "The time is short: it remaineth, that ... they that have wives be as though they had none."

It is spiritually hazardous in the extreme for a wife to leave her husband or a husband to put away his wife and for a church to approve separation. For as the apostle points out in verses 2-5 of this chapter and as Jesus warns in Matthew 5:31, 32, the likelihood is that both the one who leaves and the one who is left will take other lovers, thus falling into the sin of adultery. The one who left her or his mate will be responsible, therefore, for the perishing of the other. And the church that approves these goings-on will be responsible for the perdition of all involved.

If a wife must leave her husband for some reason other than fornication, perhaps because the man becomes drunken and beats her and the children, this leaving may take place only with the knowledge and approval of the elders of the church. Before the wife leaves, the elders will have worked with these two members of the church (and it is two members of the church that the apostle has in view in verses 10 and 11) in order to remove the sin that threatens the marriage. After the wife leaves, the elders will continue to work with the sinning husband to bring him to repentance so that the wife can quickly return.

Elders must take seriously their responsibility to take the oversight of all cases of marital trouble in the congregation, especially all cases of separation and divorce. The Reformed creed, **The Second Helvetic Confession** (1566), gave wise counsel to the church when it exhorted

> Let lawful courts be established in the Church, and holy judges who may care for marriages, and may repress all unchastity and shamefulness, and before whom matrimonial disputes may be settled (Chapter XXIX).[20]

No wife (or husband as the case may be) may simply take matters into her own hands, deciding on her own to leave and washing her hands of her husband. For the command of Christ in Matthew 18:15ff. applies to wives and husbands in the church: If your brother (husband)

---

[20] *Reformed Confessions of the 16th Century,* ed. with Historical Introductions by Arthur C. Cochrane (Philadelphia: The Westminster Press, MCMLXVI), p. 298.

sin against you, tell him his fault; if he will not listen, call in witnesses; and if he neglects to hear them, tell the church (the elders).

In such cases, as in the case of a wife's leaving her husband because of his fornication, there may be no remarriage. This is the subject of the next chapter.

Chapter 6
Remain Unmarried

But and if she depart, let her remain unmarried....
— *I Corinthians 7:11*

With express appeal to the Lord Himself, the apostle forbids remarriage after separation. He forbids remarriage in so many words in verse 11 where he entertains the possibility of a believing wife's lawful separation (divorce) from her husband on the ground of his fornication: "But and if she depart, let her remain unmarried, or be reconciled to her husband."

The wife who leaves her husband has two options, and two only. Marrying another is not an option.

This, the apostle reminds us, is the command of the Lord Jesus Himself: "I command, yet not I, but the Lord" (v. 10). During His earthly ministry, Christ not only forbade married persons to separate from their mates but also commanded those who were separated by no fault of their own to remain unmarried. This was Jesus' teaching in Matthew 5:31, 32:

> It hath been said, Whosoever shall put away his wife, let him give her a writing of divorcement:
> But I say unto you, That whosoever shall put away his wife, saving for the cause of fornication, causeth her to commit adultery: and whosoever shall marry her that is divorced committeth adultery.

The sin of the husband who unjustly divorces his wife is that he "causeth her to commit adultery." As a divorced woman, she is likely to remarry. But if she remarries, she commits adultery. Even though she was not to blame for the divorce, since she neither was guilty of fornication nor instigated the divorce, she must remain unmarried. This is reinforced by the words "and whosoever shall marry her that is divorced committeth adultery."

It may safely be inferred that the man who unjustly divorces his wife has his eye on another woman whom he intends to marry. As a pastor, my immediate response to every man who dolefully informed me of his intention to divorce his wife was, "Who is the other woman?" I cannot recall that I was ever mistaken. Implied then in the Lord's law in Matthew 5:31, 32 is that a woman unjustly divorced, whose husband is involved with and eventually marries another woman, is forbidden to remarry. The "innocent party" may not remarry.

The apostle has this aspect of the Lord's doctrine of marriage in mind when he writes in I Corinthians 7:10, 11 that it is the Lord's command that, if a wife departs, she is to remain unmarried.

The "Innocent Party"

This authoritative explanation of the teaching of Jesus on divorce and remarriage by His apostle makes plain that in Matthew 19:9 Jesus was not giving the "innocent party" the right to remarry after divorce. Elsewhere in the gospels where Jesus spoke of divorce and remarriage, He unconditionally forbade all remarriage after divorce as adultery (cf. Mark 10:11, 12; Luke 16:18). In Matthew 19:9 the Lord might seem to have granted one exception to His prohibition against remarriage, namely, in the instance that one's wife is sexually unfaithful.

> And I say unto you, Whosoever shall put away his wife, except it be for fornication, and shall marry another, committeth adultery: and whoso marrieth her which is put away doth commit adultery.

On the basis of this passage it is widely held in Protestant churches that the "innocent party" in a divorce may remarry. By the "innocent party" is meant the married person whose wife or husband has been sexually unfaithful but who has himself or herself been faithful. The right of the "innocent party" to remarry rests squarely on the interpretation of Matthew 19:9 that regards the exception clause as qualifying not only the prohibition against divorce but also the prohibition against remarrying after divorce. On this interpretation, not only may a man divorce his unfaithful wife but he may also then marry another.

One of the most influential works in Presbyterian and Reformed circles advocating this interpretation of Matthew 19:9 is Presbyterian theologian John Murray's *Divorce*.[21] Murray concludes his exegetical study of the passage thus:

> The considerations preponderate rather in favour of the conclusion that when a man puts away his wife for the cause of fornication this putting away has the effect of dissolving the bond of marriage with the result that he is free to remarry without thereby incurring the guilt of adultery. In simple terms it means that divorce in such a case dis-

---

[21]   Philadelphia, Pennsylvania: The Presbyterian and Reformed Publishing Company, 1961, pp. 33-43.

> solves the marriage and that the parties are no
> longer man and wife (p. 43).

Paul's inspired commentary on Jesus' teaching in Matthew 19:9 conclusively proves this interpretation to be mistaken. With specific reference exactly to Jesus' doctrine on divorce and remarriage in the gospels ("I command, yet not I, but the Lord," v. 10), the apostle forbids the wife who has left her husband (because of his fornication) to remarry: "Let her remain unmarried" (v. 11).

In Matthew 19:9 Jesus was giving a ground only for divorce. He was not giving a ground for remarrying after the lawful divorce. This was in keeping with the question that He was answering, "Is it lawful for a man to put away his wife for every cause?" (Matt. 19:3) The question concerned putting away or divorce. That the exception clause was intended to qualify only the prohibition against divorce is indicated by its position in the text. It immediately follows the words "Whosoever shall put away his wife" and precedes the words "and shall marry another." If Christ had meant to teach that fornication is a ground of remarriage as well as of divorce, the exception clause would follow the words, "and shall marry another." The text would then read, "Whosoever shall put away his wife and shall marry another, except it be for fornication ...."

That in Matthew 19:9 which puts it beyond doubt that Christ was not giving a ground for remarriage is the second half of the text. The second part of the text is invariably ignored by those who think to find a ground for the remarriage of the "innocent party" in the first part. With reference to the wife who has unjustly been divorced by her husband and whose husband has then wickedly remarried, Christ said, "... and whoso marrieth her which is put away doth commit adultery." Even though she is the "innocent party," her remarriage will be an adulterous marriage.[22]

Not even the "innocent party" may remarry. In the church of Christ it has been ordained that the husband may not put away his wife and that the wife may not leave her husband. If the wife does leave because her husband is a fornicator, she must remain unmarried. The same holds for the husband who justly puts his fornicating wife away.

Remarriage of the Guilty Party

One thing is indisputable. If the "innocent party" may remarry, so also may the guilty party remarry. The stand of some churches and theologians that only the "innocent party" may remarry, although it commends itself to sentiment, is in fact untenable. For if indeed the "innocent party" is free to remarry, this can only be because the original marriage bond has been dissolved. Obviously, one who is yet married may not remarry. But if the bond is dissolved for the "innocent party," it is dissolved for the guilty party as well. In the nature of the case, marriage cannot be dissolved only for one partner in the marriage. And if the bond is dissolved for the guilty party, he is free to marry again. God Himself gives him the right to marry again. All unmarried persons are at liberty to marry. Paul teaches this very thing in the wider context of I Corinthians 7: "Art thou loosed from a wife?... But and if thou marry, thou hast not sinned" (vv. 27, 28).

---

[22]   For a thorough treatment of this passage, see *Marriage: The Mystery of Christ and the Church*, 110-122. See also the appendix in *Better to Marry*.

Underlying the error of the position that the "innocent party" may remarry is the notion that sexual sin has the power to dissolve a marriage. Fornication has the power to loose what God has bound. Men and women themselves have the power to loose what God has bound. The apostle refutes this notion in verse 39 of I Corinthians 7 where he explicitly states that only death dissolves a marriage: "The wife is bound by the law as long as her husband liveth; but if her husband be dead, she is at liberty to be married ...." Only God can loose what He has bound.

The same truth is taught in Romans 7:2, 3:

> For the woman which hath an husband is bound by the law to her husband so long as he liveth; but if the husband be dead, she is loosed from the law of her husband. So then if, while her husband liveth, she be married to another man, she shall be called an adulteress: but if her husband be dead, she is free from that law; so that she is no adulteress, though she be married to another man.

Strangely, some try to escape the force of the passage by arguing that the apostle is not here speaking of earthly marriage but of the marriage of the justified and sanctified believer to Christ. As though the only authoritative teaching of the Scriptures occurs when a certain truth is the main subject under consideration! In fact, the apostle's doctrine in Romans 7:2, 3 of marriage as a lifelong bond, of the freedom of a married woman to marry another only when her first husband is dead, and of the adultery of all remarriage while an original mate is still living is extraordinarily forceful exactly because it is not the doctrine under consideration. It appears here as a truth that is presupposed and that will be acknowledged by all so that it can serve as the reality in earthly life to which loosing from the law and marriage to Christ is analogous.

If what the apostle says about marriage and remarriage in verses 2 and 3 is altogether false, as is the vehement testimony of many evangelicals and conservatives today in confession and practice, what happens to the teaching about being dead to the law in order to be married to Christ that is based on and analogous to the truth of marriage set forth in verses 2 and 3?

Paul's mention in I Corinthians 7:10, 11 of the option of reconciliation in case a wife does leave her husband points out an important reason why the "innocent party" should not remarry. She should be ready to forgive her husband if he repents of his fornication and to return to him. Fornication does not require divorce but merely allows for it.

Whether desertion of a believer by an unbeliever is ground for remarriage deserves separate treatment in the next chapter.

Chapter 7
If the Unbeliever Departs

But if the unbelieving depart, let him depart. A brother or a sister is not under bondage in such cases: but God has called us to peace.

— I Corinthians 7:15

We have seen that marriage is a lifelong bond and that those who separate or divorce are called to "remain unmarried." But does not the apostle give a ground for remarriage in verse 15?

> But if the unbelieving depart, let him depart. A brother or a sister is not under bondage in such cases: but God hath called us to peace.

It is widely accepted among evangelicals and Presbyterians, and increasingly in Reformed churches, that this text is a biblical warrant for divorcing and remarrying. A believer married to an unbeliever should stay with the unbeliever as long as the unbeliever is pleased to dwell with the believer. But if the unbeliever deserts the believer, the abandoned believer may both divorce the unbeliever and marry someone else. Desertion is a ground for remarriage.[23]

This interpretation is a complete misunderstanding

---

[23] See Murray, *Divorce,* pp. 55-78. Murray is far more cautious and restrained in finding in I Corinthians 7:15 a ground for divorce and remarriage than are most of his supposed disciples.

of verse 15. If it is understandable that men might misinterpret the exception clause in Matthew 19:9, it is a mystery that men find in I Corinthians 7:15 a ground for remarriage. For one thing, the subject is not at all the issue of remarriage. This issue is raised in verse 39. For another thing, the language itself of the text has nothing to do with remarriage. The text does not speak of a believer's being loosed from his or her mate but of the believer's not being under bondage. It does not talk of a legal right to remarry but of a condition of peace.

Desertion

The apostle addresses Christians who are married to unbelievers. Having commanded the Christian not to separate from the unbeliever if the unbeliever is willing to dwell with the Christian, the apostle must take into account the very real possibility that the unbeliever is unwilling to dwell with his now converted wife or her now converted husband and leaves. It is the unbeliever who departs. The believer does not depart. He may not depart. Verses 12-14 forbid him to depart.

> But to the rest speak I, not the Lord: If any brother hath a wife that believeth not, and she be pleased to dwell with him, let him not put her away.
> And the woman which hath an husband that believeth not, and if he be pleased to dwell with her, let her not leave him.
> For the unbelieving husband is sanctified by the wife, and the unbelieving wife is sanctified by the husband: else were your children unclean; but now are they holy.

Nor does the believer cause the unbeliever to depart by his or her ungodly behavior. If the unbelieving wife leaves because her professing Christian husband treats her brutally or if the unbelieving husband leaves because his Christian wife never ceases to preach to him, it is not really a case of the unbeliever departing but of the believer driving the unbeliever out. But the unbeliever leaves. He takes action. And he leaves exactly because he hates Christ, the life of Christ, and his wife as one of Christ's.

The deserted believer simply lets him go: "Let him depart." The believer is not to try to force her unbelieving and departing husband to live with her. She need not pursue him to the ends of the earth forever pleading with him to return. She certainly does not offer to compromise her faith in order to keep her husband.

Spiritual Peace

After the unbeliever has left, the believer is without any burden of guilt, shame, and spiritual anxiety even though she is not living with her husband. She is not responsible before God for the gross evil of the breakup of the marriage.

This is what Paul means when he writes, "A brother or a sister is not under bondage in such cases." Not being under bondage refers to one's spiritual state. It describes one's standing before God, as this is reflected in one's own experience: Without guilt! without shame! without terror!

Accordingly, the apostle adds as the exact opposite of being under bondage, "but God hath called us to peace." The deserted wife consciously enjoys peace of heart and mind. Although she is living apart from her husband, she is conscious of living in harmony with the will of God and of God's favor resting upon her. This is peace.

Being at peace, rather than being under bondage, is not by any stretch of the imagination the right to divorce the unbelieving husband or wife.

Compelling is the comment on I Corinthians 7:15 by C. Caverno in his article on "Divorce in NT," in the unrevised edition of *The International Standard Bible Encyclopaedia.*

> If Paul has treated of divorce at all it is in I Cor 7. But even a careless reading of that chapter will disclose the fact that Paul is not discussing the question for what causes marriage might be disrupted, but the question of manners and morals in the relation. Paul has not modified Christ in any respect. It has been supposed that in verse 15 Paul has allowed divorce to a believing partner who has been deserted by one unbelieving, and so he has been sometimes understood as adding desertion to the exception Christ made as cause for divorce. But Paul has not said in that verse or anywhere else that a Christian partner deserted by a heathen may be married to someone else. All he said is: "If the unbelieving departeth, let him depart: the brother or the sister is not under bondage ... in such cases: but God hath called us in peace." To say that a deserted partner "*hath not been enslaved*" is not to say that he or she may be *remarried.* What is meant is easily inferred from the spirit that dominates the whole chapter, and that is that everyone shall accept the situation in which God has called him just as he is. "Be quiet" is a direction that hovers over every situation. If you are married, so remain. If unmarried, so remain. If an unbelieving partner deserts, let him or her desert. So remain. "God hath called us in peace." Nothing can be more beautiful in the morals of the marriage relation than the direction given by Paul in this chapter for the conduct of all parties in marriage in all trials.... That neither Paul nor anyone else ever put such construction upon

his language (namely, the right to divorce and remarry—DJE), is evidenced by the fact that there is no record in history of a single case where it was attempted for 400 years after Paul was in his grave, and the Roman Empire had for a century been Christian. Then we wait 400 years more before we find the suggestion repeated. That no use was ever made of such construction of Paul in the whole era of the adjustment of Christianity with heathenism is good evidence that it was never there to begin with. So we shall pass Paul as having in no respect modified the doctrine of divorce laid down by Christ in Mt 19.[24]

Still Bound

Nor does "not being under bondage" have anything to do with "not being bound" any longer to the deserting unbeliever. Those who find here a ground for remarriage read the text as though the apostle said, "A brother or a sister is not *bound* in such cases." They imply that "being under bondage" is the same as "being bound." Usually this is not stated, much less argued, but merely assumed. But "being under bondage" and "being bound" are two different words in the Greek language, as they are in the English language. Indeed, they are two different words in I Corinthians 7. To be "under bondage" — the word used in verse 15 — is the Greek word *doulooo*. To be "bound" — the word used in verse 39 — is the Greek word *deoo*. It is perfectly apparent even to one who is completely ignorant of the Greek language that these are two, distinct words. When the Holy Spirit inspires "*doulooo*" in verse 15, therefore, we may not

---

[24]   James Orr, ed., Volume II (Grand Rapids, MI: Wm. B. Eerdmans Publishing Co., 1960), pp. 865, 866.

translate or interpret as though He had moved the apostle to write "*deoo*."

With characteristic disregard for the very words themselves of the Scriptures, the New International Version translates I Corinthians 7:15 thus: "But if the unbeliever leaves, let him do so. A believing man or woman is not *bound (sic)* in such circumstances; God has called us to live in peace." By one stroke of some translator's pen, the marriage bond is dissolved by the leaving of one's mate, and Christians are freely permitted to remarry while the original mate is still living. "A believing man or woman *is not bound.*" But the pen of the translator has falsified Holy Scripture. Holy Scripture does not say "is not bound," but rather "is not under bondage." Holy Scripture will stand.

These two distinct words express two sharply different ideas. To be under bondage is to be a slave. In the Scriptures, this slavery may be spiritual, as in Galatians 4:3, or physical, as in Acts 7:6 and in I Corinthians 7:21. To be bound to someone is to be joined to her in a close relationship in which also there are obligations. I am bound to my wife; I am not under bondage to her (nor, since ours is a Christian marriage, is she under bondage to me). When the apostle speaks of the relationship between a wife and her husband in verse 39, he does not use the word "*doulooo*" ("The wife is under bondage ... as long as her husband liveth") but the word "*deoo*" ("The wife is bound ... as long as her husband liveth").

Desertion by an unbeliever, although it leaves the abandoned believer in spiritual freedom, does not dissolve the bond of marriage so as to give the believer the earthly liberty to remarry. Though not under bondage, the deserted believer is still bound.

This is driven home in verse 39: Only death dissolves the bond! Only God dissolves the bond by means of death! Treating the issue of remarriage expressly, answering the question "When may the believer marry another than her original husband?" the Word of God declares: "if her husband be *dead*"; "*only* if her husband be dead"; "if her husband be dead *in actual fact.*" Only when one's husband or wife is dead is one "loosed," as the apostle expresses it in verse 27, so that there is no sin in marrying again.

Marriage is a lifelong, one-flesh bond established by God as earthly symbol of the unbreakable covenant of grace between Himself in Christ and His wife, the church. This determines all marriage thinking and marriage practice in the church.

Summing up, the apostle ordains in all the churches:

1) that Christians are to live faithfully with their mates, no matter how difficult this may be;

2) that Christians are not to desert, separate, leave, put away, divorce;

3) that there is, however, an exception to the forbidding of leaving or putting away, namely, the fornication of one's mate, as was taught by the Lord Himself;

4) that even in this case remarriage is forbidden;

5) and that one important reason for not remarrying is to leave open the way for reconciliation. This is always the Christian option since reconciliation is the way of God in Christ with His wife, the church, and with each member of the church personally.

Practical Implications

We conclude this study by briefly taking note of several practical implications of the teaching of I Corinthians 7 on desertion, divorce, and remarriage.

First, obedience to the ordinances laid down in the passage will mean suffering and loss for some Christians. There is nothing particularly surprising about this since all the commands of the gospel mean hardship for some disciples of Christ. The life of discipleship in this present world is a life of self-denial along a narrow way.

Second, the preaching of these ordinances by the church will spare the saints the guilt and heartache of divorce. It will preserve many marriages and homes. It will guard the people of God against their eternal destruction. These commands are good, healthy, and beneficial. It is sheer folly that pastors fail to preach them and that elders neglect to make them their admonition.

Third, the stand of a church that accords with these ordinances will serve well the children of the church, the holy, covenant children. The children will rise up and call their mother, the church, blessed for her protection of them through these ordinances.

Fourth, this stand brings the church into conflict with the deserting, divorcing, remarrying, fornicating world. But it also brings down upon the church that is obedient to her Lord the ridicule and rage of the unfaithful, departing churches, which always have a good word for deserting, divorcing, and remarrying.

Fifth, taking and maintaining this stand against desertion, divorce, and remarriage is not a matter of being unsympathetic to the afflictions of the people. Rather, it is a matter of being submissive to God's ordinance of marriage. A monogamous, permanent bond between one man and one woman is what marriage is by divine appointment. The church did not decide this. God did. The church cannot change this anymore than she can change the law of gravity. The church does not make the laws governing the lives of the saints. She merely explains and applies them.

Sixth, for those who have already broken God's law concerning marriage, whether by fornication, by an unbiblical divorce, or by remarriage, there is a way of escape from condemnation. This way is repentance. Repentance finds forgiveness in the atoning death of Jesus Christ. There is abundant mercy in the Savior to blot out the guilt of fornication, desertion, divorce, and remarriage. But repentance breaks with the sin and walks henceforth in obedience to the ordinances of God, regardless of the cost.

If someone says, "But Jesus would never require someone to live a lonely life or to forego the pleasures of marriage and family," I respond, "You do not yet know either Jesus or the reality of discipleship." Jesus' apostle raises the very real possibility of a life of loneliness as the result of his doctrine of marriage in verse 11 of I Corinthians 7: "But and if she depart, let her remain unmarried ...." In the context of His rigorous prohibition of divorce and His absolute prohibition of remarriage, Jesus Himself said, "There be some who have made themselves eunuchs for the kingdom's sake" (Matt. 19:12).

To every one of us who proposes to follow Him as a believer, the Lord says, "If any man come to me, and hate not his father, and mother, and wife, and children ... yea, and his own life also, he cannot be my disciple. And whosoever doth not bear his cross, and come after me, cannot be my disciple.... So likewise, whosoever he be of you that forsaketh not all that he hath, he cannot be my disciple" (Luke 14:26ff.).

Those who are happily married should honor their marriage for Christ's sake, enjoying it and using it to the glory of God.

But if marriage would prevent someone from following Christ now and from enjoying the real marriage hereafter, let him or her despise marriage, also for Christ's sake.

For the time is short. Let those who have wives and husbands be as though they had none, and let those who have no husband or wife be as though they had a Friend who is better than a husband or a wife. For the fashion of this world, including earthly marriage, passes away. Then those who have obeyed the Lord, suffering loss, forsaking houses, brothers, sisters, father, mother, wife, children, and lands for Jesus' sake shall receive an hundredfold, and shall inherit everlasting life (Matt. 19:29).

Appendix

The Remarriage of the "Innocent Party" — A Sermon

And I say unto you, Whosoever shall put away his wife, except it be for fornication, and shall marry another, committeth adultery: and whoso marrieth her which is put away doth commit adultery.

— Matthew 19:9

Scandal

It is painfully evident to everyone that the dishonoring of marriage in evangelical Protestant churches today is scandalous. Divorces for every reason and remarriages abound. It is now lawful for a man to put away his wife for any cause and to marry another, often someone else's wife, and to be a member in good standing in an evangelical church.

The causes of this scandal are many. For one thing, the churches are conformed to this world. In North America we live in a society in which one of every two marriages breaks up in divorce and in which it is acceptable to remarry. Like Israel under the Old Covenant, the churches have learned well the ways of the heathen among whom they live.

Another cause is the silence of the pulpit and the neglect of the key-power of Christian discipline. Due partly to their sympathy for the hard lot of some members and due partly to their fear lest they cause trouble in their congregations, ministers refuse to preach the truth about marriage, divorce, and remarriage, and elders refuse to exercise censure upon members who sin in the matter of marriage.

Not long ago, a deeply disturbed church member related to me that he had gone to his minister pleading that he teach the congregation the will of God concerning marriage. He had made this plea because of the abominable events that were occurring in the congregation. Members were divorcing their own wives and husbands and remarrying each other's wives and husbands. The minister's response was, "I would not touch that subject with a ten-foot pole."

At the International Council on Biblical Inerrancy held in Chicago, Illinois, in 1986, where inerrancy was to be applied to the Christian life, some proposed a strong statement on the lifelong nature of marriage, condemning divorce except in the case of fornication and forbidding remarriage. Pastors of the large evangelical churches opposed the proposal vehemently since it would have created trouble in their churches, filled as they are with divorced and remarried members. Needless to say, the proposal got nowhere.

Fundamentally, the cause of the scandal is that the churches refuse to bow, unconditionally, to the sovereign authority of the Holy Scriptures. When the Pharisees asked Jesus about the lawfulness of divorce, He replied, "Have ye not read?" that is, "What does the Bible say?" "What does God say in His inspired Word?" (Matt. 19:4) What God said "at the beginning" in Genesis 2:24 was decisive for Jesus as regards marriage and divorce. Not so for the evangelical churches. Neither what God said about marriage at the beginning nor what God said about marriage in Matthew 19 is the rule for marriage, divorce, and remarriage in evangelical churches today.

The consequences are dreadful.

Divorce and remarriage are destroying Christian families by the thousands. Countless wives and husbands, wickedly divorced by their mates, and multitudes of children, abandoned by one of their parents, are ruined. They are ruined psychologically, spiritually, and eternally.

Worse still, divorce and remarriage disgrace God's Name. People called by the name of the God who is faithful in His covenant are unfaithful in the most basic of all the relationships of life. Their claim is that the God of Christianity justifies and approves this gross unfaithfulness. They ransack His Word to discover warrant for their violation of their sacred vow of marriage. When they remarry, often another man's wife or another woman's husband, they do so in a Christian ceremony, using an obliging minister of the gospel, and with yet another pledge of godly fidelity. It is common in evangelical churches that this is repeated three and four times. This is a profaning of the name of God.

It is urgent that the true church of Christ and her faithful ministers bear witness to God's truth concerning the unbreakable bond of marriage.

The "Innocent Party"

A serious challenge to this testimony about marriage is the claim that the "innocent party" in a divorce has the right to remarry. The "innocent party" is the faithful

husband whose wife commits adultery against him or
the faithful wife whose husband wickedly divorces her
for another woman. Some who oppose other remarriages as unlawful have great difficulty with the prohibition of the remarriage of the innocent party.

People are naturally sympathetic to the innocent
party and suppose that the Scriptures would make
allowances for them and their need.

But there is also biblical argument for the position
that the innocent party may remarry. Appeal is made to
Jesus' words in Matthew 19:9. Although Jesus forbids
divorce and remarriage, there is an exception: "except
it be for fornication." Surely, say the advocates of the
remarriage of the innocent party, this establishes the
right of the innocent party to divorce his or her unfaithful mate and to marry another.

Marriage, then, is not a lifelong, unbreakable bond.
Men and women can break it. They can break it by
fornication.

This popular understanding of the text, however, is
mistaken. The text itself makes plain that the remarriage
of the innocent party is forbidden by the Lord.

Scripture Interprets Scripture

If there can be a question whether the innocent party
may remarry, there can be no question that the remarriage of all others is forbidden. Assuming for the
moment that in Matthew 19:9 Christ permits the innocent party both to divorce and to remarry, He definitely
forbids all other divorce and remarriage. All remarriage following a divorce that is not due to fornication is
adultery. All such remarriage is continuous adultery, as
the present tense of the verb, "committeth adultery,"

indicates. There is one, and only one, exception to Christ's prohibition of remarriage after divorce: The fornication of one's wife or husband.

This, then, is what the church must teach. The members of the church must make this the rule for their marital life. The elders must enforce this rule with Christian discipline.

Even this would be a rather strict stand on remarriage. Few churches, if any, take this stand. With rare exception, those that once did take this stand, the Reformed churches in the Dutch tradition, have long since opened the doors to divorce and remarriage for every reason.

Our concern now, however, is exactly to examine the assumption that in Matthew 19:9 Jesus permits the innocent party to remarry. The interpretation of verse 9 that permits the innocent party to remarry suffers the very serious handicap from the outset that it conflicts with the teaching of the Scriptures in other, clearer passages. The interpretation that gives the innocent party the right to remarry goes like this. Jesus is forbidding remarriage. To remarry after divorce is adultery. But there is one exception to this prohibition of remarriage: The fornication of one's mate. If one has divorced his wife because of her fornication, he does not commit adultery when he remarries.

According to this interpretation, the exception clause "except it be for fornication" qualifies both the divorcing and the remarrying. It gives the man the right not only to divorce his unfaithful wife but also to marry another woman.

It is a basic rule for sound interpretation of Scripture that a passage must be explained, not all by itself, apart from the rest of Scripture, but in the light of other passages that are similar. It is an even more basic rule that the passage that is less clear must be explained in light of the passages that are more clear. This is the meaning of the great Reformation principle "Scripture interprets Scripture."

Matthew 19:9 is not the only passage in the New Testament on divorce and remarriage. There are several other passages. Among the passages treating remarriage after divorce, Matthew 19:9 is the least clear. The reason is the presence of the exception clause in a statement that forbids both divorce and remarriage. It is not perfectly clear from the first part of the text what it is to which Jesus intends to give an exception. Does He intend to allow for an exception only to the prohibition against divorce? Or does He intend to allow for an exception as well to the prohibition against remarrying?

It is understandable that some raise the question whether the innocent party may remarry, if they look only at the first part of Matthew 19:9. But we may not look only at Matthew 19:9, much less only at the first part of this text. We must look also at the other, clearer passages.

First, there are the passages that clearly forbid all remarriage after divorce without any qualification or exception. Such is Mark 10:11, 12:

> And he saith unto them, Whosoever shall put away his wife, and marry another, committeth adultery against her. And if a woman shall put away her husband, and be married to another, she committeth adultery.

In Luke 16:18 Jesus teaches the same:

> Whosoever putteth away his wife, and marrieth another, committeth adultery: and whosoever marrieth her that is put away from her husband committeth adultery.

All remarriage after divorce is condemned as adultery. There is no exception.

The apostle of Christ forbids any remarriage after divorce when he teaches that marriage is a bond that is broken only by the death of the husband or the wife. This is his teaching in I Corinthians 7:39:

> The wife is bound by the law as long as her husband liveth; but if her husband be dead, she is at liberty to be married to whom she will; only in the Lord.

What must be noticed about this text is that the subject is precisely that of the lawfulness of remarriage. The question faced by the apostle is "When is a married woman at liberty to marry another man?" The perfectly clear answer of the apostle is "Only when her husband dies." The reason given is that marriage is a lifelong bond.

In Romans 7:2,3, having stated the same fundamental truth about marriage, Paul draws out of this principle, explicitly, the implication that whoever remarries while her first husband is still living is an adulteress:

> So then if, while her husband liveth, she be married to another man, she shall be called an adulteress: but if her husband be dead, she is free from that law; so that she is no adulteress, though she be married to another man.

Another passage that bears on our understanding of Matthew 19:9 is Matthew 5:31,32:

> It hath been said, Whosoever shall put away his wife, let him give her a writing of divorcement: But I say unto you, That whosoever shall put away his wife, saving for the cause of fornication, causeth

her to commit adultery: and whosoever shall
marry her that is divorced committeth adultery.

This passage helps us to understand Matthew 19:9 in
one important respect in that it clearly teaches that the
fornication of one's wife (or husband) is a valid ground
for divorcing her (or him). Fornication is the one biblical
ground for divorce. Our question concerning Matthew
19:9, remember, is whether the exception clause is intended to qualify only the prohibition against divorcing
or also the prohibition against remarrying. Nowhere
else do the Scriptures teach that fornication is a ground
for remarriage. Rather, the Scriptures elsewhere teach
that all remarriage after divorce is adultery. But Matthew 5:31,32 does teach that fornication is a ground for
divorce. This would lead us to suppose that in Matthew
19:9 the exception clause must be taken to qualify only
the prohibition against divorce.

No Remarriage

A careful examination of the Lord's words in Matthew 19:9 reveals that this is exactly His teaching. This
is evident from the placement of the exception clause in
the text. The words "except it be for fornication"
immediately follow the words "whosoever shall put
away his wife" and precede the words "and shall marry
another." The exception applies to the prohibition
against divorce. Had Jesus meant to give an exception
to His prohibition against remarriage, He would have
placed the exception clause after the words, "and shall
marry another." The text would then have read, "Whosoever shall put away his wife and shall marry another,
except it be for fornication," etc.

The deliberate placement of the exception clause

following the mention of divorce but preceding the mention of remarriage indicates that Jesus is giving an exception only regarding the prohibition against divorce.

That Jesus is not teaching that the innocent party may remarry is proved conclusively by the second part of the text: "and whoso marrieth her which is put away doth commit adultery." It is a serious violation of a basic law governing the interpretation of the Scriptures that men ignore the other, clearer passages on remarriage in their explanation of Matthew 19:9. It is an even worse error that they commonly ignore the second part of the text itself.

The second part of the text refers back to the wife of the first part. Her husband has divorced her even though she was not guilty of fornication. He has since married another and, according to the judgment of Christ, is living in adultery. The woman referred to in the second part of Matthew 19:9, therefore, is the innocent party. According to those who find in the first part of the text the right of the innocent party to remarry, she should be free to marry another man. But Christ denies this: "Whoso marrieth her which is put away doth commit adultery." Even though she is the innocent party, she may not remarry. If she does, her marriage is an adulterous marriage.

The doctrine of the Lord in Matthew 19:9 then is this: Husbands may not divorce their wives. If they do, they sin. The rule in the kingdom of Christ is that expressed in verse 6: "What therefore God hath joined together, let not man put asunder."

There is one exception to this forbidding of divorce: The fornication of one's mate. Fornication in the text is sexual unfaithfulness to one's husband or wife in that one has sexual relations with another. Usually, it is adultery, but it refers as well to homosexual sin.

Fornication is the one biblical ground for divorce. This brings home to Christians the importance of sexual faithfulness in marriage and the gravity of the wickedness of adultery. It also brings out that the wisdom of the Lord is practical. No one is required to live with a fornicating mate with all the dangers to soul and body that this involves.

There is an exception to the prohibition against divorce. There is no exception to the prohibition against remarriage. All who remarry after divorce, regardless of the fact that they are the innocent party, commit adultery. The guilty husband who has divorced his faithful wife and married another commits adultery. But also the man who marries the innocent divorcee commits adultery.

Interpreted in this way, Matthew 19:9 harmonizes with the teaching of Christ and His apostles elsewhere in the New Testament, that marriage is for life and that all remarriage after divorce is adultery. It also accords with the fundamental Word of Jehovah God about marriage in Genesis 2:24 to which Jesus has referred in verses 4 and 5 of Matthew 19: "... For this cause shall a man leave father and mother, and shall cleave to his wife: and they twain shall be one flesh."

This explanation fits the context, for the question of the Pharisees concerned divorce, not remarriage: "Is it lawful for a man to put away his wife for every cause?" (v. 4). Jesus is answering the question "Are there grounds for divorce?" He is not answering a question about grounds for remarriage. Jesus mentions remarriage because remarriage is invariably in view when a man divorces his wife.

It may be noted that this interpretation of the text, with its prohibition against the remarriage of the innocent party, was the virtually unanimous position of the church for about a thousand years after the apostles.

The Ground of the Prohibition

The ground of the prohibition against the remarriage of the innocent party is simply what marriage is by the sovereign act of God the Creator. Marriage is a lifelong, unbreakable bond between one man and one woman. Jesus had taught this basic truth about marriage in verses 4-6 of Matthew 19:

> And he answered and said unto them, Have ye not read, that he which made them at the beginning made them male and female, And said, For this cause shall a man leave father and mother, and shall cleave to his wife: and they twain shall be one flesh? Wherefore they are no more twain, but one flesh. What therefore God hath joined together, let not man put asunder.

In teaching this, Jesus points out that He was only repeating what God Himself had revealed about marriage on the occasion of His institution of marriage in Paradise. In Genesis 2:24 God Himself had revealed that His institution of marriage is an indissoluble bond for life.

At issue in the controversy over the remarriage of the innocent party is the very nature of marriage itself. Is marriage merely a conditional contract hammered out between a man and a woman — a contract hammered out in the presence of God but still only a contract between the two? If this is what marriage is, it can indeed be broken by the failure of one or the other to fulfill the basic condition of the contract, namely, sexual faithfulness.

Or is marriage not a contract at all but a relationship, a union, made by God? And is it such a union, such a divine joining, of the two that they become one flesh? If this is what marriage is, it cannot be dissolved by man. The state cannot dissolve it; churches cannot dissolve it; society cannot dissolve it; the married persons themselves cannot dissolve it. Only God *may* dissolve it. Only God *can* dissolve it. God dissolves it by death. Christ's forbidding of the remarriage of the innocent party rests on the conception of marriage as an indissoluble bond formed by God. Verse 9 of Matthew 19 is grounded in verses 4-6.

Even though her husband has unjustly put her away and entered into an adulterous marriage with another woman, the innocent woman may not remarry. Whoever marries her commits adultery. For she has a husband. He is a wicked husband. He is living in adultery with another woman. But he is her husband. She is bound to him. God binds her to him. God binds her to him until death as they no doubt acknowledged when they married, vowing "until death us do part."

If, on the contrary, the innocent party is free to remarry, the guilty party is likewise free to remarry. Some like to restrict the right of remarriage to the innocent party. But this is impossible. If the innocent party in a divorce may remarry, the reason must be that the marriage has been dissolved. No one, except perhaps an unreconstructed Mormon, would allow a person who is presently married to marry another. The guilty party has dissolved the marriage by his fornication. But if the marriage is dissolved for the innocent party, it has been dissolved also for the guilty party. In the nature of the case, a marriage cannot be dissolved for only one of the married persons anymore than a marriage can be an adulterous marriage for only one of the persons. This means that the guilty person is no longer married. In this case he is free to marry, for God gives every unmarried person the right to marry if he wills (cf. I Cor. 7:27, 28).

Permitting the innocent party to remarry necessarily opens the church up to the acceptance also of the remarriage of the guilty party. Two examples reflecting that which is actually happening in evangelical churches will make this clear.

A man's wife leaves him to whore around with other men. He divorces her on the biblical ground given in Matthew 19:9. According to the stand of his church, the man — the innocent party — then remarries. Later, the unfaithful wife repents and returns to the church. When she desires to remarry, the church must approve. For her original marriage was dissolved by her fornication. As an unmarried woman, she has every right to marry. In addition, her original husband has been allowed to remarry so that reconciliation with him is impossible.

Or a man divorces his wife unbiblically in order to marry another woman. The innocent woman remarries with the blessing of the church. Later, the original husband professes repentance and seeks admission into the church with his second wife. The church must approve his present marriage and receive the couple since his original marriage was dissolved by his adultery.

Christ approves none of this. The remarriage of the guilty party is continuous adultery: "(He) committeth adultery." Also the remarriage of the innocent party is adulterous: "Whoso marrieth her which is put away doth commit adultery." For Christ honors His own institution of marriage as an unbreakable bond. God ordained marriage in the beginning to be the earthly symbol of His own relationship of love with His people in Christ. The reality of marriage is the covenant of grace that God has established with Israel/church. God married Jerusalem according to Ezekiel 16. The fulfillment of this marriage according to Ephesians 5:22ff. is the New Testament covenant between Christ and the church. Marriage is the "great mystery... (of) Christ and the church" (Eph. 5:32).

God is faithful in the covenant. He never divorces and remarries. God is faithful at awful cost. He gave up His only begotten Son to the death of the cross. By the atoning death of the Son of God, faithless Israel/church obtained the right to be God's bride. On the basis of the cross, the Spirit of Christ cleanses Israel/ church so that she becomes faithful to God in thankful love.

Jesus Christ taught a doctrine of faithfulness in an indissoluble marriage bond because He practices this Himself in the real marriage.

Some Practical Implications

This must be the stand of the church that is determined to teach the nations "to observe all things whatsoever I have commanded you" (Matt. 28:20). Her stand on remarriage is determined by the doctrine of her Lord as revealed in the Scriptures. This must be her stand regardless of the culture in which she lives; regardless of the teaching and practice of other churches; and regardless of the opposition within her own membership of fathers, mothers, brothers, sisters, and friends of those who desire to remarry.

Christ's stand on remarriage conflicted with His culture and with the practice of the Jewish church. No one took the stand that He did. This dissuaded Him not at all. All that mattered to Him was the will of God: "Have ye not read, that he which made them at the beginning made them male and female, and said... What therefore God hath joined together, let not man put asunder."

The church's stand includes calling all remarriage after divorce adultery. This is not the unforgivable sin. But with this sin as with all other sins the one way of forgiveness is the way of repentance, and repentance is a heartfelt sorrow that breaks with the sin.

The prohibition of the remarriage of the innocent party will mean hardship, loss, and suffering for some of God's people. There will be innocent parties who forgo the pleasures and comforts of marriage and family. But it is a mistake to argue that Jesus would never require anyone to give up sex, marriage, family, and home. Immediately after He has taught that marriage is a lifelong bond (vv. 4-6) and that, therefore, there may be no remarriage after divorce (v. 9), Jesus applied His doctrine to the life of the citizens of His kingdom by noting that "there be eunuchs which have made themselves eunuchs for the kingdom of heaven's sake" (v. 12). Some are indeed called by Christ to deny themselves with respect to sex and marriage.

The trouble is that evangelical churches at the end of the twentieth century either have forgotten or deliberately hide from their members that it belongs to the very nature of the Christian life that it is a life of self-denial, not self-fulfillment. Christ reminds His disciples of this in verse 29 of Matthew 19:

> And every one that hath forsaken houses, or brethren, or sisters, or father, or mother, or wife, or children, or lands, for my name's sake, shall receive an hundredfold, and shall inherit everlasting life.

But grace is given to those called to deny themselves sexually so that they "receive this saying" (v. 11), and there will be a reward (v. 29).

As for the objection that the prohibition against the remarriage of the innocent party is proved wrong because it allows the wicked (the guilty party) to injure the righteous (the innocent party), the entire Christian life is an exposure of the saints to injury at the hands of the ungodly. They are slandered, cursed, persecuted, and killed all the day long, as well as divorced unjustly by husbands and wives who are worse than infidels (I Tim. 5:8). All this they must bear patiently for Christ's sake, waiting for the Day of Christ when the Lord will reward them and avenge them of their cruel enemies.

The truth of the lifelong nature of marriage impresses upon all who marry, especially the young people, that they marry carefully and wisely. Christians must marry in the Lord. They must marry someone who has the same view of the sanctity of marriage that they do.

Implied also is that all married Christians live together from day one of their marriage in the love of God, obeying the will of Christ for husbands and wives, practicing Christian marriage, working at making their marriage a living symbol of the blessed, peaceful, delightful, exciting union of Christ and the church, and reconciling with each other at the cross on the very day that they have a falling out. In this way, divorce and remarriage will never even enter their minds.

Obviously, Christ's forbidding of remarriage warns married persons against divorcing their wives or husbands and marrying another. To do this is to inflict the most grievous wound upon one's mate. In addition to all the anguish of the abandonment and of the knowledge that one's own wife or husband is in the arms of another, the divorced person is shut up to a life of loneliness. What is still worse, divorcing one's wife exposes her to adultery and damnation because she will be tempted to remarry. This motivates Christ's warning against divorce in Matthew 5:31,32: "Whosoever shall put away his wife, saving for the cause of fornication, causeth her to commit adultery." Divorce and remarriage are hatred of that neighbor to whom love is due more than to any other.

This is the word of the Lord Jesus Christ.

Admittedly, it is a hard saying. His disciples found it so: "If the case of the man be so with his wife, it is not good to marry" (Matt. 19:10).

Christ's response?

"He that is able to receive it, let him receive it" (v. 12).

Amen